Soundings

C000092271

Special Issue

The Next
Ten Years

EDITORS
Stuart Hall
Doreen Massey
Michael Rustin

POETRY EDITOR
Carole Satyamurti

REVIEWS EDITORS
Becky Hall and
Susanna Rustin

ART EDITOR
Tim Davison

EDITORIAL OFFICE
Lawrence & Wishart
99a Wallis Road
London E9 5LN

MARKETING CONSULTANT
Mark Perryman

Soundings is published three
times a year, in autumn,
spring and summer by:
Soundings Ltd
c/o Lawrence & Wishart
99a Wallis Road
London E9 5LN

ADVERTISEMENTS
Write for information to Soundings,
c/o Lawrence & Wishart

SUBSCRIPTIONS
1997-8 subscription rates are (for three issues):
UK: Institutions £70, Individuals £35
Rest of the world: Institutions £80, Individuals £45

ISBN 0 85315 854 1

Text setting Art Services, Norwich
Cover photograph: © Nicholas Garland

Printed in Great Britain by
Cambridge University Press, Cambridge

CONTENTS

Notes on Contributors   *v*

Editorial: What Next?
Michael Rustin   7

Let's Get Engaged: relationships between people and government
Sarah Benton   19

A Coming Constitutional Revolution
Anthony Barnett   28

Northern Ireland the Union and New Labour
Mary J Hickman   35

Tackling Regional Inequality in Europe
Ash Amin   53

Poem
Carole Satyamurti   68

A New Gender Contract?
Jean Gardiner   69

Getting Food Right
Tim Lang   77

The Man in the Ford Sierra: What the New Government's Transport Policy Should Be
Kerry Hamilton and Susan Hoyle   88

Law and Order in the 'New' Britain
Bill Bowring   100

The Unions and New Labour
Gavin Poynter   111

What Health Tells Us About Society
Richard Wilkinson   125

NOTES ON CONTRIBUTORS

Nicholas Garland is a cartoonist working at the *Daily Telegraph*

Sarah Benton writes, edits, researches and lives in London

Anthony Barnett was the founding Director of Charter 88. He now directs the Sovereignty Seminar at Birkbeck College London

Mary J Hickman is Reader in European Studies and Director of the Irish Studies Centre at the University of North London

Ash Amin is Professor of Geography at the University of Durham

Carole Satyamurti is poetry editor of *Soundings*

Jean Gardiner is Senior Lecturer in the School of Continuing Education at the University of Leeds, and author of *Gender, Care and Economics* (Macmillan 1997)

Tim Lang is Professor of Food Policy at the Centre for Food Policy, Thames Valley University

Kerry Hamilton is Professor of Transport Studies at the University of East London

Susan Hoyle is an independent writer and consultant, and a Research Associate at the Transport Studies Unit at the University of East London

Bill Bowring is Senior Lecturer in Law, and Director of the Pan-European Institute at the University of Essex. He is International Secretary of the Haldane Society of Socialist Lawyers

Gavin Poynter lectures in the Department of Innovation Studies, University of East London, and formerly worked in the Education Department of the TUC.

Richard Wilkinson is Senior Research Fellow at the Trafford Centre for Medical Research, University of Sussex, and author of *Unhealthy Societies: The Afflictions of Inequality* (Routledge 1996)

What Next?

When a new government - our government - has just been elected, the relationship to it of its long-term supporters is inevitably an intense one. Are the hopes which have been placed in it justified? Do its early decisions give grounds for celebration and trust, or are they on the contrary a cause for anxiety, and for remembering breaches of values between previous Labour administrations and their various constituencies. The reality was bound to be, and is, complex and contradictory. But the emphatic change signalled by the landslide victory, and the capacity shown by the new government on many fronts to seize its moment, signal a large political opportunity, and it is in the hope of contributing something to this prospect that this special issue of *Soundings* has been prepared.

The challenge now, however, is to think constructively about the next ten years (as we hope it will be), and neither to celebrate nor anguish unduly about every immediate decision the government takes. The question for a magazine like *Soundings* is how to understand the forces and tendencies which will shape this future, and which are not always visible in day-to-day political exchanges, or recognised by focus groups (even by a giant focus group of 5000 members such as has been proposed by Tony Blair).

What is the significance of the fall of the Thatcher regime? Is New Labour's historical mission merely to give a kinder face to the counter-revolution which Thatcherism imposed, or does it signify an opening to a different balance of social forces? One can read the situation in both these ways, and this is perhaps its essential ambiguity.

The Conservative governments of the 1970s and 1980s became committed to dismantling much of the post-war settlement - that system of institutions and social programmes whose main object was to protect working people against the turbulence and risks of markets, whilst still maintaining a dynamic capitalist economy. (It should not be forgotten that the economic growth rates of the 'Great Boom' of the period from 1950 to 1975 far exceeded those which have been achieved since: it is far from the case that the 'Welfare State' inhibited capitalist development in the West.)

These forms of social defence included, among other things, the organised strength of the trade union movement, whose membership has fallen during the past twenty years from 12 million to 7 million; a system of progressive taxation which succeeded, until the early 1980s, in achieving a diminution of inequalities of wealth and income in Britain; and a large and powerful public sector, which provided a zone of protected and secure employment, and which had the effect of limiting disparities of income and wealth - the culture of 'downsizing' and self-aggrandizement which has followed privatisation shows up by contrast the modest but real achievements of the 'old' public sector in representing different values. The fourth form of defence was the 'welfare state' itself, the system of protection and opportunities made up of the National Health Service, public housing programmes, pension provision, and education. The Major government fell at the point when this last bastion of the universalistic post-war system of protection was entering its terminal crisis, as funds became (deliberately) too depleted to maintain adequate standards within the public system, and pressure was placed on ever-larger numbers of citizens to make provision for themselves, according to their individual resources. The Major government fell largely because this creeping dismantling of the welfare system was experienced as one ideological step too far. A large majority voted for the continuation of universal health care, adequate educational provision, and an enhancement of their security, and against a culture of unrestrained self-enrichment.

But we all know, of course, that New Labour has committed itself not to reverse most of the changes introduced by its predecessor governments. It is an unusual feature of New Labour's political strategy that it is been more bold in stating what it will *not* do, than in setting out its positive commitments. New Labour has, like the Clinton Democrats in the United States, been running as strongly against the shadowy presence of a 'left alternative' to itself (roughly, Old Labour) as it has against its Conservative Party adversary. The rebuilding of the public sector, the restoration of the privileges of the trade unions, and the use of taxation to achieve a greater measure of social equity and a different balance of public over private goods, have all been disavowed as conceivable or even as desirable policy-objectives. Labour's strategies in the welfare field are yet to be fully revealed, though their likely direction is not difficult to predict.

The grounds for this policy-shift, which goes far deeper than the earlier revisionisms of the Crosland-Gaitskell era, were of course largely the imperatives of political survival. The working class was believed to have become too small a social fraction to provide the core of an electoral majority, a political judgement which had early legitimacy conferred on it from the left in Eric Hobsbawm's 'The Forward March of Labour Halted?' article of 1981. But New Labour also became convinced that the post-war system had become unworkable. The arrangements which had brought a measure of social protection for the vast majority were now thought to be too authoritarian and paternalistic in their assumptions, and to deny the opportunities for choice and self-definition which were so temptingly displayed in so many new market places in the 1980s and 1990s (for those, that is, who had resources to bring to those markets). In its critique of the Old Labour system, New Labour was greatly assisted by the analysis of the new left of *Marxism Today*, which both identified 'Thatcherism' as a new and threatening claim to hegemony, and showed why some of its appeals to the people now had to be taken ultra-seriously by its progressive adversaries. New Labour sought power on the assumption that Galbraith's 'culture of contentment' - the complacency of the two-thirds society now indifferent to the fate of the other third - now ruled, and that overt challenge to it would mean political suicide.

But these adjustments to political reality - the endless antitheses of 'New' and 'Old' dignify this with the idea that these adjustments represent 'modernity' itself - leave large unanswered problems. How can populations be protected against the effects of markets - those engines of inequality and insecurity - without the kinds of 'countervailing powers' - of progressive taxation, universal social provision, a large public sector committed to public goods, and strong trade unions - which were previously constructed for just this purpose? What *other* instruments, perhaps more 'modern' ones, does New Labour have in mind to develop to do the work of these outmoded agencies? The problems of inequality, exclusion, insecurity, polarisation, have not after all gone away - these are what have given victory to Labour even in the midst of a minor economic boom. Only the solutions to them seem to have disappeared.

Nevertheless, within the constraints it has imposed on itself, New Labour has said that it remains concerned about what it now defines as 'moral' evils. It has tried to identify remedies for social injustice, to give substance to its claims to stand for a different moral agenda. Just as it proposed, before and during the election campaign, a 'windfall profits tax' to generate work for the young unemployed, so it found in its first budget a 'contingency fund' to enable the health and education services to get through the next twelve months without visible disaster. But the limits the government has set for itself are very tight, measured against the scale of the problems, and against the natural disposition of market forces to increase inequality and exclusion. *Something* can be done in crucial marginal spaces by these means. But not much, in the long-run, to solve the problems of social polarisation and an underfunded welfare system that are the products of the last twenty years.

There is a faint echo of theoretical debates from the 1970s in New Labour's insistence that it subscribes to 'moral' definitions of social problems, and rejects 'economic determinism'. In reality, only a tiny sect of Althusserian Marxists ever sought to deny that inequality and injustice *were* moral problems, or insisted that understanding their ultimate material causes was *everything*. This tendency never achieved a large political influence in Britain .[1] But what is as absurd as the denial of an ethical dimension to inequality and injustice is the rejection of the idea that these conditions do also have economic and systemic *causes*, and cannot be remedied unless these causes are addressed. Yet those who appear to hold this preachers' view that ethics are everything are not an obscure and defeated theoretical sect, but the dominant tendency in the New Labour government. The article in this issue by Bill Bowring describes the implications for the field of law and order of an approach which operates mainly in the register of blame, tough on crime but not on its causes.

It is another paradox that a political leadership which now stakes everything on the ethical has been comprehensively denounced by the leading survivor of the traditional Labour right, Roy Hattersley, for having altogether given up its concern for inequality and poverty (in *The Guardian*, 26 July 1997).

---

1. Some will remember the severe battering this position received from Edward Thompson, in his essay *The Poverty of Theory*.

We should make clear that we do not advocate a return to a lost paradise of 1960s or 1970s welfarism, corporatism and statism. The historic moment which generated this unstable class compromise has plainly passed. It was in the end the deep polarisations upon which this compromise was based, which ran from top to bottom of Britain's deeply class-structured society, which brought about its failure. The demands of the International Monetary Fund on the one hand, and the members of much of the British trade union movement on the other, proved impossible to reconcile through the fragile structures of Wilsonian corporatism.

We hold, however, that many of the issues and instruments of this earlier class settlement remain relevant. Articles in this special issue (by Richard Wilkinson and Gavin Poynter respectively) make a strong case for the centrality of equality and inequality as measures of social well-being, and for the necessity of a strong trade union movement to support employees in the otherwise unequal contest between capital and labour. But whilst we hold that 'Old Labour' traditions and commitments should not be written out of the script, we also believe that new scripts are needed. A new social narrative, with contemporary actors, is going to be necessary if the promise of a post-Thatcher era is to be realised. The problem is to discern what the shape of this should now be.

The cause of public versus private goods has only been successfully fought in political terms when it has been grounded in real experience and fact. Galbraith's critique of 'private affluence and public squalor' articulated one such moment, for the 1960s. Just as the theorists of the market had to reinvent, in the 1980s, the case for market systems and what they could achieve for individuals and societies, so advocates of the 'social' and 'public' need now to be comparably innovative and original within their own frame of values.

It must not be forgotten that the Thatcherites developed genuinely new ideas and perceptions. They realised, for example, that for many the market was an emancipatory, liberating force, giving a sense of empowerment against what was perceived as a ruling class located in the state bureaucracy and among the educationally privileged. Thatcherism became the ideology of class fractions, including many individuals of working-class origin, who felt that their opportunities were being enhanced by the newly-liberated market. It is from this that its self-confidence and sense of righteousness derived. The radical, anti-establishment, vulgar, often envious tone of the Thatcherite reformers in confronting what they saw as established privilege struck chords with rising as well as declining classes. Thatcherism both embodied the resentment of those whose worlds were being undermined by the forces of change (as all conservative movements do), *and* the hopes and expectations of some fractions who saw new routes to advancement. Even in the public services, such as health, 'managers' gained whilst 'professionals' lost, each claiming in self-justification that they represented the true public interest. It was this double appeal, which looked backwards to a lost imaginary plenitude, and aggressively forwards to new opportunities, which accounted for the success of the New Right.

The largest evidence of this success, and a melancholy vindication of the theory of 'Thatcherism', is that in its rise it largely converted its New Labour opponents to its own ways of thinking.

The Thatcherites invented 'internal markets' within the public services, demonstrating that it was possible to introduce pressures for greater efficiency, responsiveness to demand, and internal diversity within systems which remained still recognisably public. It seems unlikely that the old bureaucratic monoliths of public sector provision will ever be wholly reinstituted in the light of these changes. Greater elements of choice and empowerment for consumers of public services, and a more devolved operational and budgetary responsibility for their supply, seem likely to be permanent goals of any viable public system. Whilst the particular dogmatic architecture of internal markets, with their wasteful transaction costs and undermining of common purpose, will need to be radically rethought, it is unlikely that anyone would want the welfare sector - whether in health, housing, social services, or education - restored to the status quo ante of 1979.[2]

Recasting the 'public' and 'private'

A damaging split between the 'public' and 'private' domains has been called in question by the reforms of the past twenty years, and this draws attention to other splits which were both basic to the welfare state, and a source of its underlying weakness. The antithesis of altruism (public) and egotism (private), of production (private) and welfare (public), also came close to being an

---

2. The *Soundings* theme issue on the 'Public Good' (4, Spring 1997) explored some new ideas on these questions.

antithesis of the unequal domains of men (those who were said to produce the resources in the sphere of production and markets) and women (those who were deemed to spend what was allotted to them in the home and in the welfare sector).

The recasting of this division, already far advanced through the ending of gender inequality in educational access and outcomes, and through the large-scale entry of women into the workforce (though still on far from equal terms) has been a major transformation. The imposition on to the public domain of 'rational imperatives' of efficiency and responsiveness to consumer demand might seem less of a capitulation to the market than it has done, if we could achieve also a countervailing absorption by the 'private sector' of values and norms hitherto antithetical to it, of social and environmental responsibility. The 'socialising' of the private - for example through the ideas of 'stakeholding' advanced by Will Hutton and others, and perhaps through some actualisation of 'ethical' dimensions in relations with employees, customers, environments and future generations - could be the other side of a necessary reintegration of public and private spheres. Whilst 'altruistic' values were allotted mainly to the 'dependent' sectors of home and welfare, and 'egoistic' values commanded the productive sphere, the contest between these value-systems was always going to be an unequal one.

Thatcherism saw itself as an invasion and conquest of what was then thought of as the 'public domain' by capitalism. The privatisation of the public utilities, one of Thatcherism's other exportable inventions, has indeed had just this quality and intent. We wish to redefine this process as potentially just one moment in the dissolution of a long-standing antithesis between the public and the private, in which the private was always the dominant force. Three articles in this issue, by Tim Lang, Kerry Hamilton and Susan Hoyle, and Jean Gardiner, show how these boundaries need to be rethought in specific terms, giving substance to the view that it is through particular cases and areas of social experience that these questions will be advanced, not through taking up *a priori* ideological positions.

Food, for example, has seemed to consumers as if it wholly belonged within the private sphere, in its modes of production, distribution, and consumption. (The supermarket is one of the icons of the age, also the location of some of its most visible economic and spatial transformations.) But, of course, food never was a private matter. Agriculture, both nationally, and later on a European scale, is one of the most highly subsidised of industries, though these subsidies have in no way protected the agricultural labour force in Britain from virtual extinction. Food has always required regulation, for purposes of public health. Recently, as Tim Lang shows in his article, the BSE crisis has exposed this vital public interest in the chain of food production and distribution. The operations of this industry, and the need to subject it to some more normative and democratic regulation, turn out, unexpectedly, to be as significant for the direction of the society as energy supply was earlier.

Transport is another emblematic case. The continued expansion of the motor car as the primary mode of transportation is plainly becoming unsustainable. Its costs, in human death and injury, are in any case insupportable. Its ecological implications, given global industrialisation, are extremely serious. Its effects on the social life and cohesion of cities are also becoming damaging. This is not a matter of ideology - the majority who own, or who have through their families regular use of cars, know what benefits and pleasures they confer. But the unsustainable effects of increasing car ownership have to be recognised. Public transport, so ideologically hated by Thatcher, has now to be rebuilt and reinvented, with some of the social priorities which Kerry Hamilton and Susan Hoyle's article suggests.

And thirdly, on the other side of the established divide of ostensibly public and private provision, and requiring a substantial extension of the 'public', is child care. Equal opportunities for women, and improved opportunities for disadvantaged children, will not be secured without, in this sphere, a major extension of the public sector in a sphere now largely left to families and voluntary self-help.

The politics of individualisation

The old 'mass constituencies' of Labourism are no longer available as agents of progressive social transformation. In the strange 'class society without classes' in which we now live, it seems unlikely that class identities can now be reinvented as major vehicles of social action. One reason for this is that class identities seemed to embody the very inequalities of status which socialist ideologies sought to challenge. Thatcherism brought off the feat of making intolerable the subjective recognition of inequality, even as it made substantive inequalities worse. The strength of Labour's former coalition depended on forms of hierarchy and control - in the trade union movement, in the party, and in the larger culture, which are no longer acceptable in a society fragmented by consumerism, and by a much greater sub-cultural diversity and autonomy. So prospective agents of democratic transformation have to be rediscovered anew.

This is the deepest problem facing New Labour and the prospective radical coalition elected in May 1997. Individualisation has penetrated deeply. Whilst this is sometimes described as simply an aspect of an inevitable 'modernity', we regard it more as a new discourse of power. 'Individualisation' has been achieved in part politically, through a regime which has deliberately thrown responsibility on to individuals.

The attack on 'welfare dependency', the insistence on individual (and parental) responsibility, the advocacy of 'welfare to work', the development in the public sector of systems of appraisal, quality audit, performance related pay, and fixed-term contracts, the growing disparity of rewards and incomes, are all individualising devices designed to weaken social solidarities. Individuals were to - and did - learn, that their destiny depended on themselves, not on what society could do for them. This also legitimated a reduced sense of obligation to support the well-being of others. Why should individuals do as much for society, if society was not going to do as much for them?

Thus the development of a tax-aversive society. In place of progressive taxation to support improved public services - each of these foresworn for the first two years of the new government - we will find an emerging culture of payment required only for specific services. Whilst one democratic element of this concept of 'hypothecation' is to provide a greater transparency of connection between taxation and the expenditures made possible by it, its more central purpose is to ensure that those who make contributions themselves receive the benefits. A ubiquitous insurance principle supplants the idea of the obligations and benefits of social membership.

The proposals made by the government for higher education reform, following the report of the Dearing Committee (which was set up with bipartisan support) is the first example of New Labour's implementation of this principle of self-funding welfare. Instead of young people's education being funded by taxes paid by the parental generation, the young are to be obliged to find some of the costs from a mortgage taken out against their own future earnings. They thus become educated in the ways of a consumerist, individualised, society: what you receive, you must pay for yourself. Parents will of course go on supporting their children through college. The difference is, that it will now only be their own children, not other people's, that they will support.

One effect of these measures, like the earlier withdrawal of social benefits from 16-18 year olds, is to impose strain on families, and to increase the relative disadvantage of those whose family structures are fragile. It will become relatively easier for those families with resources, both material and other, to pass on their advantages to their children, and relatively harder for children from those families without them. The effects of these measures on equality of opportunity, and thus on inequalities in the next generation, will be negative.

Of course, the present system of higher educational funding is inequitable, in its treatment of graduates as compared with non-graduates. Some years ago, one of the editors of *Soundings* proposed an alternative more comprehensive system of support, in which all young people of 18 years of age would be entitled to two years of free post-school education, whether this took the form of a degree course or a vocational course. A system of universal educational credits, not confined to those achieving A-level qualifications (the Robbins Report standard), would be a more egalitarian way for society to provide generously for its next generation.

It seems likely that Labour's forthcoming reforms of the pensions system, under the influence of Frank Field, will go down the same 'contribution-related' road. By these means, citizens are encouraged to believe that the market is sovereign, and that provision for old age, higher education for one's children, and perhaps eventually all education for one's children, and health care too, are to be funded by individuals making provision in the appropriate market-places.

And if you can't make this provision? Well, prepare for a great deal of moralising talk and re-education, whose ostensible aim is to get you into a condition where you can. And whose ulterior aim is to convince the rest of society that it is all your own fault.

Rebuilding Social Solidarities

The majority of the British population, it seems, did not like the look of the society which was emerging under successive governments ruthlessly committed to the market, nor the high individual risks of insecurity and impoverishment that were attached to it. The problem is to see how the 'old' solidarities, which supported the earlier more-or-less comprehensive systems of social protection, can now be complemented by new ones. This issue of solidarity and membership (which is raised in different ways for Continental societies whose solidarities have been based on social Catholicism) is the crucial question for the next political decade. If new concepts of social membership, and a willingness, for their sakes, to inhibit individual gains do not emerge, Britain will go down the American road. The 'learning from Clinton' that we have already noted (in *Soundings* 4) as a principal source of New Labour's political technology, will also become the main line of its accommodation to capitalism.

One new ground of solidarity lies in the emergence of new political subjects, and the revitalisation of the democratic process that has taken place in reponse to the authoritarian politics of Thatcherism. It is in this sphere that New Labour's agenda remains most radical. Four articles in this special number address these issues. Anthony Barnett discusses the importance of constitutional reforms as elements of what he sees as a genuine modernisation of the British State. Mary Hickman, writing about Northern Ireland, notes the ways in which received concepts of 'Englishness' and 'Britishness', taken-for-granted throughout this lengthy crisis, may now be undergoing genuine contest and change. The recognition of a greater diversity of legitimate cultural and national identities, within whatever state structure can be negotiated into existence, may be the basis of a solution which even some Unionists may now be perceiving. This argument plainly has relevance for what may happen once a Scottish, and perhaps a Welsh, Assembly, come into being, leading to alternative grounds of social identification. Ash Amin's article on Europe raises related issues on a larger plane. Whilst a European Union merely intended to enforce market disciplines on a Continental scale will be of little benefit, regional devolution and diversity within a strengthened Union would be a worthwhile objective. Finally Sarah Benton raises the question of the kind of relationship which might develop between New Labour and its publics, in despite of New Labour's evident preference at this point for the relationship of performers to audiences, or advertisers to a voiceless public. One thing which we will certainly have to re-learn, if the promise of the next ten years is to be realised, is a capacity for dissent and opposition.

Who can say whether citizens enabled mainly as consumers, released from the subordinating as well as supportive constraints of class identities, and with more education and access to communication than ever before, will now merely accept the roles cast for them by the corporations which are now the world's most powerful institutions? If socialists were ever right in their conception of human needs and human nature, this world of consumption seems unlikely to be humanity's final destination.

The aspiration towards membership, towards goals and values which transcend individual interest, is a deep-seated one. It is notable that the Thatcherites finally found themselves at war with concepts of social purpose located not only in trade unions, universities, and hospitals (where one might have expected to find them), but also in the judiciary and among the prison governors. At the end of the day, there did seem to be something called society after all.

We think the issue is an open one. Just as the Thatcherites evolved their programme, in response to social aspirations and forces whose strength they only gradually came to recognise, so our aim must also be to seek to identify such an agenda of possibility. The changing boundaries of the public and private, the 'stakeholding' debate, the recognition of plural identities and communities, and a renewed vitality to democratic politics, all already provide elements for such an agenda. We know that they are not sufficient to transform New Labourism. We also think that facing up to what we do not yet know is a political necessity.

This issue of *Soundings* publishes articles which offer some solid perspectives on our political prospects. They begin this new phase of political debate.

MR

Let's get engaged

Sarah Benton

Blair's team has a unique purpose: to lower demand. This is one half of the key to his promise, some years ago, to create a feasible socialism. Smaller expectations might actually be met, meaning there could be actual changes in how we live that would be wanted, worked for and welcomed. By reducing hope, hope might be increased.

In the old language of high hope and grave disappointment, it is the left which has 'betrayed' the people by suggesting, piously, that a radical, universal egalitarian socialism is achievable in our times. Excising the tattered icon of that hope - Clause IV - from the heart of Labour was Blair's first step to creating the politics of New Labour, just as the prize of excising it was clumsily pursued by the Labour right during the 1950s.

Does Blair's team then hold in common with Crosland, Gaitskell and Jenkins nothing more than the cynical, amoral timorousness of British social democracy through the decades?

Some of the team, may be. And the anti-inflationary aim of that old social democracy is part of New Labour's heritage. New Labour's 'new' socialism follows directly from the 1978 Dimbleby lecture, when Roy Jenkins argued that the two party system was fatally damaging to good government; each party had to distance itself from the other and each outbid the other with unrealistic promises it couldn't keep. The process engendered disappointment, an inevitable cry of 'we've been betrayed', and mutual cynicism of electorate and politicians. It produced bad politicians and bad citizens who behaved liked peevish children. Jenkins (who did not use those words) was manoeuvring into the argument for a third party, the Social Democratic Party that was created three years later, flaunting its 'political virgins' as new model citizens.

You'll have to start from here

Whatever the outcome, Jenkins and Blair shared a starting point: to achieve good government, party, party leaders and citizens have to change, and the first step is to change political discourse from a language of dreams and wish-lists into one of realistic expectation Both men have wanted to drive out dogmatic idealism - the 'I wouldn't start from here' excuse - and replace it with engagement with what is. Of course, all then depends on what is engaged with and by whom.

A policy of engagement between citizens and providers will have to be embarked on by both government and public service managers. The language of reducing expectations is already the language of the public services - for, contrary to political myth, politicians rarely shape the state; rather they shape the discourse of what the state has the capacity to do. The left's belief in the omnipotence of the state was born, not in the marxism of the nineteenth century, but the wars and revolutions of the twentieth, when - and only when - a state quickly evolved with the totalising power and unlimited budget to do the impossible. That experience and potential only recently faded; no-one wanted to acknowledge how much it owed to war. The sharp party differences of the 1980s did not reflect autonomous party processes so much as the crisis of the state, burst open by the winter of discontent. New Labour is the vehicle for the modern political discourse of the limited national state. The SDP was the forerunner of this, using its Liberal connection to cast back to pre-war structures (but unable to contain the destructive ex-Labour rage against the Labour left.).

Choice, judgment, self-help, scarcity, rationing, protection, fairness, consent - this is the state-based discourse New Labour has to shape. Where there is abundance, leave it to the market; where there is scarcity, the state is still required to ensure a modicum of social justice. Without a new way of engaging people in judgment about justice, then government has only one message: persuading people to wait, to want less. As Margaret Thatcher recognised, once the language of commerce is applied to public services - give me more, give me what I want, give it now - the clients of the service cannot but feel betrayed and accusatory. Her response was also to change the citizenry, to reconstitute it by stripping it of its civic ownership of public utilities. In the end, the only civic virtue remaining was to be a good, authoritarian parent; knowing how to say No.

If we don't hear a new discourse in New Labour, about us as well as government, then the new civic values are the bleakly familiar ones of restraint and rationing, of not wanting, not asking, of the management of scarcity and the restraint of impatience and frustration - but only for those without large disposable private incomes. But if instead we explore the idea of engagement, then change becomes feasible; and if we kick over the coy silences and pseudo-reverence about money - who gets what, how they spend it - then a new civic practice becomes possible. It would be nice to think that this is what Amitai Etzioni, the 'communitarian', and Tony Blair talked about in their private chat in June.

Blair's other half

This is where the other half of the key to Blair's promise of a realisable 'social-ism' (his stress) comes in. It is the idea of ethical socialism, in which some process of moral regeneration changes our experience of life simply because we are re-invested with the qualities of faith, hope and love which have atrophied during decades of cynical and materialistic socialism. A fortnight into the new government, nowhere was this dual message more clear than in the health service: 1) no pay rises, no extra money; 2) nonetheless all is changed because staff and client/citizens are infused with new hope and faith. Perhaps it's true; perhaps waiting 12 months for a new hip under New Labour will be indeed less irksome than waiting 12 months under couldn't care less Tories. Though not for long.

This recovery of Christian/idealistic socialism from the 1880s is contingent on the turns of history, and the turn of history which New Labour is riding has carried them away from the long wrestle with Marxism. The anti-clause-IVism of the 1950s and 1960s was never part of a moral crusade; it was repugnant in part because it was constructed, not as a means to achieving something good, but as a weapon to combat the quasi-marxism of the Labour rank and file, especially those who were close to the Communist Party. Crudely, the anti-clause-IVism of that time was part of its time, of the cold war, of all political initiatives being corralled, spuriously, into a pro-Soviet, pro-Marxism, pro-ideological politics camp or a pro-American, anti-ideological, anti-idealistic camp. Freed from the rigid strictures and structures of the cold war, political idealism can now find new homes - or float vacuously and die.

So one feature of New Labour which makes it different from old-style right-wing Labour, or old-style social democracy, is that it has not been moulded as a block against Marxism or the Communist Party. For the first time ever, there is a

Labour government which is not at war. This has been extremely discomfiting. It's not just that most of us are only too aware of the many enemies of an even minimal social justice and equality; those of us who are political also drank in the language of conflict and hatred as the language of politics with our first meeting. Which is precisely of course why so many, more women than men, dislike politics. Where there is no conflict, no belligerence, where is the politics?

Is there a politics to be constructed out of friendly, judicious co-operation, and if so will we the punters play the game or, like the SDP's 'political virgins', will we have no role but to worship?

Is it really love?

The words that poured out of Labour's inner circle meant little to us who were schooled in the language of 1970s Marxism. Class, state, hegemony, battle, power - no, not so much key words as ways of mapping the world, understanding its dynamics. However, as foreign as the discourse of ethical, and particularly Christian, socialism - or indeed, any form of religious politics - is to us non-believers, squirm as we may at words like God, love and spirit in political discourse, a refusal to take these beliefs seriously will be our loss. We will fail to understand where Blairite politics are coming from, and we will mistake the silence of what cannot be spoken in public (eg, God, love, faith) for absence of intent.

After Blair's first speech as leader to the Labour Party conference (1996) I came home and counted up how many times he'd used the word love. I forget now, but it was a lot. Two would have been a lot in the love-lost terrain of British politics, but it was a lot more than that. Since then he's added more: hope, faith, trust - service. Service was, from the 1880s to the 1940s, the central concept of citizenship for Idealists.

Remove the particulars, though there have been precious few of those, and the language could come straight from the platforms trod a hundred years ago by those Idealists - Liberal and Christian socialists - who did so much to shape a distinctive British socialism. These were not the methodists of the early nineteenth century; the 'idealist' or 'ethical' socialists were of High origin - high Church, high University. They had a mission, which was to educate, educate, educate, and they are found in the University settlements (Toynbee) that were set up for intellectuals to engage with workers, the adult education movement (Tawney was the first tutor and President of the WEA) and Oxford University itself (AD Lindsay, TH Green).

The idealism foundered not on a lack of willing intellectuals or workers to pursue the higher good, and practice good fellowship, but on the fastidious reluctance of many intellectuals to put their minds at the service of workers in conflict. The number who shared the essential combined commitment to transcendent spirituality and social justice was also too small against the weight of established and economic labourism. Ominously too (for their heirs today) they could create no consensus on capital and property. A man's property remained sacrosanct. Finally, the first world war demonstrated that the capacity of the state to drive all before it made midgets of transcendent Idealists.

I f education, education, education was the means of improving society, of bringing in social justice, it was not an aim in itself. What Blair has in common with them is the idea of moral regeneration; individual people would be brought into themselves (truly decent people) by the repossession of the basic Christian virtues. However, the possession of these virtues is not an individual act; it is a product of relationships. No politician, however pious or, indeed, truly virtuous, has suggested how political action can cause one person to love their neighbour. The only initiatives on neighbours in the last ten years have all been to do with rights, the law and mediation to achieve compromise. I am writing before Jack Straw publishes his Crime and Disorder Bill, but nothing this self-proclaimed Christian Socialist said before the election suggested that he plans to discard punitive law as a response to nasty neighbours, and to pursue the path of forgiveness and charity. Perhaps the post-election proposal to make young miscreants say sorry does, however, embody a notion of virtuous relationships, and of engagement between the hitherto antagonistic virtuous victim and vicious criminal.

The idea of a virtuous circle linking government, people and state officials is on a different plane from the regulated commercial relationships of the market, and indeed of the nexus of rights and duties which has underpinned political society since the war. The welfare state of 1945-51 was not constructed on the notion of citizen rights; the idea of rights grew more slowly, partly shaped by political ideas, partly by the attempts to negotiate scarcity. John Major followed Thatcher's wasting of the civic ideal with a desultory return to rights-based citizenship. This was the Charter episode, of encoding our various rights and duties in relation to public goods. However, it was transparently an effort to police the work of 'front-line' staff by remote control and on the cheap. If anything, it has made relations between users of services and suppliers more acrimonious and intolerant.

Daddy's favourite

There is action government can take to improve neighbour relations. Just half an hour in a council housing office, Jobcentre or casualty department shows you the genesis of much of the behaviour that causes such social pain. It is here, rather than in the family as such, that people learn that they can't have what they need, that patience and courtesy only ensure you're left at the bottom of the queue, that you can't afford to take No for an answer; it is a world without grace, and riddled with the suspicion that it operates on the basis of favours, offered on some opaque system. In this graceless world much energy is spent trying to work out who gets the favours and why, what trick you might pull to get yourself to the front of the queue. Tricks and deceit get you what you need, not honesty; violent rudeness seems the only honest expression of intolerable frustration.

If the first claim of New Labour is that it has a mission to educate, the second is that it will reform the welfare state. The new post-war welfare state was constructed on the patience of the citizens. The government, the new kindly father, would put in the money and the system of care and protection; the citizens would also contribute money, but above all they would put in their patient waiting time and accept the advice of their betters. Unlike New Labour, the 1945 Labour landslide was powered by enormous expectation. It had been preceded by several years of preparation - discussions on reconstruction carried out by the Army Bureau of Current Affairs, adult education institutes and voluntary associations. That Labour government needed the energy of expectation, but wanted no more of citizens than their patience while they set about fulfilling what they could of the hopes. But patience is exhaustible and does not supply new energy, as Labour found out in 1951.

Blair's team are clearly determined not to reproduce the destructive relationships of the past. If they don't raise unrealistic hopes, they can't be bitterly accused by sulky citizens of betrayal and favouritism. The symbolism, at least, of limited promises to cut hospital waiting time, make more social housing available, leave people less long in the benefits queue, is important.

But this clearly does not change the status of people as citizens in relation to the government, though it may mitigate the bitterness. Any improvement in the quality of public services is worth having, especially for those so used to putting up with the worst. But it does not touch the idea of civic regeneration which lurks in many New Labour pronouncements, and which Blair seems to hope will spring forth naturally if not blighted by disappointment and the arrogance and hypocrisy of government. That is, faith and hope, if not charity, will be renewed if re-energised by education, and if the worst distortion and blocks of the human spirit are removed.

Money money money

The test of seriousness about new civic practice is whether or not government simply reverts to a preachy practice of telling the poor to be good or whether it starts talking about money - who gets it, and for what, what do they spend it on, where and how? If we're talking civic obligation, what is the particular obligation of the rich - OK, comfortably off - to spend their money in ways that contribute to the social good? While John Major's notion of the good citizen seemed to amount to no more than not dropping litter and turning up for your NHS appointment on time (ie, primarily defined in terms of the obligations of the non-rich), can there be a new notion of the civic obligations peculiar to those who have more than enough money to spend? Will Gordon Brown put his fiscal policy where his heart might be supposed to be, and try to lure money from property and currency transactions, into socially useful production?

In theory too, a more realistic appraisal of what government can do, and should do, could make us more *communally* self-reliant. There is now a new, if small, body of peripatetic professionals who 'facilitate' processes of learning and engagement amongst tenants and in workplaces. Frank Field, whose appointment to the Department of Social Security has delighted and unnerved observers in equal proportions, is another committed Christian. From this, perhaps, stems his less-known commitment to the idea of self-help groups running their own insurance provision - again, a direct link to the early ethical socialist belief that communal self-reliance created better fellowship and better citizens than paternalistic state protection.

The model of the self-help, campaign or community group which has entered a 'learning curve' from the moment it sets about changing things is, in fact, far more challenging than any party or state official would like. The test of the new relationship in feasible social-ism is how far such groups will be encouraged and empowered by government; how far we (citizens, voters) will take the opportunity of this change to create and develop our powers of judgment and initiative; state office holders will put themselves *at the service* of self-help and do-it-yourself groups.

Yet even if the government are transformed from being our masters into our servants, the first beneficiaries will be the master/servants themselves; that is, they will be better people if they are imbued with the idea of service. It doesn't touch the rest of us. Missing from all this, as it has been missing from the history of Labour and the civic ideal, is the idea of self-government. (Blair was inept when he made a link between Scottish self-government and English parish councils; but in fact, the inter-war Idealists frequently took the ancient English village as the archetype of self-government, from which the tradition of British democracy - sturdy men of good judgment - had developed.) They are inching towards it backward, not just with devolution for Scotland and Wales (raising the inevitable cry of 'what about England?'), but also every time any Blairite uses the concept of 'consent.' How is consent secured? How actively is consent sought? Who, on any one issue, is entitled to demand that their consent is secured?

To shift from passive, childlike dependence on government is one step towards transforming the relationship of governors and governed. Connected is the shift towards that vital civic virtue of exercising *judgment*. Judgment is the quality which the Tatton Conservative Association so conspicuously refused to exercise before the election. To take refuge in the mantra 'innocent until proven guilty' is merely to defer the exercise of judgment to the formal court. The exercise of collective judgment does more than anything else to exercise people's civic virtues. It is one of the primary justifications of jury service. It is the most potent recommendation of the 'Oregon experiment', when voters in Oregon state, USA, were asked to discuss, and vote on, the range of medical services that might be offered in a rationed system.

Unless Labour can turn round and face full-on the myriad of occasions when communal consent *and* judgment is demanded - for medical services, school provision, the use of green space and public transport a - new virtuous circle of governed, state officials and government cannot be created. Unless there is a new practice of engagement with our fellow citizens, formally and informally, we shall continue bemoaning to People Like Ourselves the descent into anomie.

That is, if we can't find a way of making New Labour an opportunity for us, not just our squeaky clean governors, we shall be left, like children, watching in wonder to see what new goodie New Labour will put out of the hat. And Blair's team, instead of practising their new dogma of responsible change, will be under intolerable pressure to continue to making us gasp with wonder at the tricks they can perform.

A coming constitutional revolution

Anthony Barnett

The Queen's Speech, or rather - for the event was in spirit republican - the announcement of Tony Blair's 1997 government programme, will be seen as historic. For the first time, a Labour administration has set about its task by changing the way in which Britain is governed as well as trying to deliver new policies. We can enjoy a doubly welcome event, therefore. Delight that the Tories were so justly thrashed, and pleasure that Labour is no longer in awe of Establishment routines.

The result, which everyone can feel, is that *we can build a new Britain*. During the election the hope became a cliché. The cliché then turned stale in our mouths, as dry and sticky as advertising gloss. Suddenly it tastes good. One could almost write that it is 'the real thing' had not wretched advertisers plundered the language of discrimination. Nonetheless, society will be less divided and fairer in terms of opportunity than it would have been under Conservative rule. There will be better growth, and a redistribution of power that may even ensure such gains are lasting. A profound and far-reaching transformation of sovereignty in Britain has started to unfold. In two plain if multi-syllabic words, a constitutional revolution has begun.

The argument was put clearly enough in Gordon Brown's Crosland Lecture a month before the election was called: the basic principle - 'Everyone should have the chance to bridge the gap between what they are and what they have it in themselves to become' (this is an astonishingly ambitious objective); the practical justification - 'what is right on ethical grounds is, in the 1990s, good for the economy too'; and the means -

Political reform is central to this: it must enable people to have the chance to participate in decisions that affect them. This is about more than the concept of a classless society, it is about power and therefore about a truly democratic society.

So we should see our constitutional proposals - which range from abolishing the hereditary principle in the Lords to devolution of power and free information - as part of a programme that makes sense of people's aspirations by redistributing power from the state, or any other vested interest, to the people themselves.

Such reform can still go wrong, of course. It is easy to conceive of ways it can be sabotaged, the legislation impaired, its energy sapped, momentum halted.

Clever Tory opposition is less likely than Labour reluctance and half-heartedness. This could hand the opposition easy targets; then procedural ambush and media corrosion can reverse the process. In effect, the lure of absolute sovereignty will have drawn the teeth of reform. For at least one thing is clear from the professionalism and determination of the leading players in the Blair Cabinet. If they want to carry through constitutional reform they have the cultural capacity to do so. This is the essential qualification. It was one lacking from the generation of Wilson and Callaghan. Despite their technical ability to manipulate the machinery of politics, mentally they were prisoners of the old regime and its wartime presumptions. Unlike them, the new Labour leaders understand the arguments for reform. Blair, for example, has given perhaps the most eloquent calls for Freedom of Information in British political history. Both he and Brown have called for a new 'constitutional settlement'. Whatever the phrase might mean, in both detail and totality they are at ease with the call for reform. Blair and Brown's reluctance to embrace proportional representation should not be regarded as a typical, Labourist blinkered tribalism. Not only they will have read and heard the arguments of Robin Cook, as well as Peter Mandelson's advocacy of AV; they are more in the line of *Marxism Today* than of Fabian pamphlets. Wilson saw the Labour Party as a bicycle that had to be pedalled faster - he would rather have fallen off it than turned it into a hegemonic project, which, indeed, is what happened.

An equally profound reason for the *possibility* of constitution reform being undertaken with success this time is the failure of the Conservative scare campaign before and during the election. I knew it would fail when I watched the six hour debate on the constitution opened by John Major on 20 February. Concluding for the then Government, Michael Forsyth denounced Charter 88 'waffle'. The one thing that the Charter cannot be held responsible for, however, is the waffle factor. When we initiated the appeal in the offices of the *New Statesman* in 1988, on the 300th anniversary of the revolution of 1688, we did so with a cogent, well-written call. It brought together those who wanted a Scottish parliament, electoral reform, a bill of rights, freedom of information or independent local government. The Charter made the links and demanded a democratic written constitution. At the height of the Lawson boom, when Mrs Thatcher's government was carrying all before it, Charter 88 was more than a protest - it offered an alternative when Thatcher claimed 'There is no alternative'.

Much to our astonishment first five and then ten thousand people added their names and we set about trying to create an organisation that would last. We were told by commentators, *C'est magnifique mais ce n'est pas la politique*. Putting it in French made their acquiescence to convention seem like wisdom. Received wisdom has a sell-by date, however, which its reproducers frequently ignore. Constitutional change soon became part of politics.

In June 1996, John Major's speech-writers drafted a speech of the then prime minister, clearly based on reading publications from Charter 88. 'Well I don't claim to be a constitutional expert', John Major declared,

> But I am a politician and a citizen, and it is from that practical experience that I want to address the issues. Because the constitution is not, to me, simply a matter of institutions - Parliament, the Crown, our legal system. At its heart I believe it's about individuals and individual freedom. How we influence and control the kind of nation we live in. The Constitution is shorthand for our rights and our democracy.

It reads strangely, does it not? A Conservative leader telling us he is a citizen and that our constitution is about our rights and democracy and what kind of a nation we are... 'What constitution is that, then?' would not be a stupid response. For around seventy years, the conservatives of Britain *have* been telling us that the constitution is a technical matter, that it is *not* something sensible people are interested in, or that practical-minded, 'ordinary' people need to bother their heads about. Naturally, this made the country much easier to govern. Today's scoffing is merely the latest echo of a thousand Pall Mall clubland jeers deriding and patronising the unwashed.

At the last quarter of an hour, historically speaking, John Major saw the constitutional writing on the wall. He sought to *appeal to the people* to save the old order. To do so, he had to use the language of democracy. But this is the language of the new - at least it remains so in the United Kingdom. This language still has little purchase on the popular imagination and almost none on those who defer to the old order. Major went on to defend the House of Lords, dragged in the monarchy, emphasised the sacred role of the House of Commons. You merely need to impress his description of the constitution back into his call to defend it, to see that it cannot be sustained. 'We must defend the House of Lords - shorthand for our rights and our democracy'. Major is using the language of reformers, terms like citizenship, rights, freedom, to defend an unreformed constitution from reform. Little wonder that his argument, if it deserves to be flattered with that description, sounded weird.

Stranger still, Major's language was as right as his use of it was wrong. The constitution *is* shorthand for our democracy - that is, our lack of it. It does concern individual freedom, national power, public accountability and common identity. A great force has pressed the issue into British politics and will keep it there. Europe forced sovereignty into British politics. Scottish demands for a parliament express a European process. Legal rights will be implemented in the first instance by the incorporation into domestic law of the European Convention of Human Rights. Decentralisation and a more independent, and - I would argue - accountable, central bank are continental style measures.[1]

But, so far Labour has backed away from putting its reforms together into a coherent programme of renewal. It has separated the parts of its reform programme, giving responsibility for each to separate departments. It has declined to provide any overall meaning to the changes it is introducing.

In this sense, the influence of reform movements like Charter 88 remains unfulfilled. The Charter's aim, certainly, was to give such specific changes a larger meaning and connect them. In this it deliberately defied Britain's political routines. These separate issues from one another in the name of pragmatism. In fact this is

---

1. I argue this at length in *This Time*, to be published by Vintage later this year.

not practical wisdom, rather it is a way of evading accountability. Take the idea that at the senior level the country is exceptionally well governed by men with 'Rolls-Royce minds'. Then count the debacles, from the invasion of Suez in 1956 to the Poll Tax and BSE. Something wrong, surely, with a system that permits such disasters? But what is this system? It has no formal existence. Our constitution has remained unwritten because this helps to protect the vested interest of the administrative state. It relies on gentlemen's agreements because this is in the interests of the gentlemen involved. It allows procedure, convention, funny names, and 'self-regulation' to be a substitute for accountability. All the executive has to do is smile and disappear up its royal prerogative.

All of which makes constitutional reform hard to understand in England. In Scotland and Wales, where parliaments will represent those countries as a whole, the constitutional culture is different. Specific reforms in England do not have this unifying character. That they might do so eventually was prefigured in the publication of the 'Joint Consultative Committee on Constitutional Reform' on 5 March. A ponderous sounding document, it listed the agreements worked through by Labour and the Liberal Democrats on reforming our political system.

In effect it argued that proceeding step-by-step is the best route to success but this needs a sense of overall direction. Otherwise, when fog descends you are likely to end up walking in circles. And our present constitution generates tons of fog. It could be fatal to proceed into it piecemeal, one reform at a time, looking backwards rather than towards a destination. The Joint Committee's concluding paragraph read:

> The proposals set out in our Report are presented as distinct measures yet they are closely related. Through them runs the common thread of empowering the people. To make this clear the new Government should make an early declaration setting out the principles behind its programme of constitutional reform and outlining the more open and modern democracy it seeks to create.

The document's opening paragraphs give an idea of what these principles might be. A society that is open and free ... power accountable to the collective wishes and interests of the people ... equal rights and responsibilities ... guaranteed civil liberty, social cohesion and economic opportunity.

We need such a statement of principles. It would transform the constitutional debate. The English would start to see what the whole thing is about. Then they will begin to believe it can happen. It will also make it easier for the government to pace its reforms one by one without charges of betrayal or sell-out.

It was when I read this paragraph that I thought that the support and effort that has gone into Charter 88 may have worked. Again, caution is the watchword. The document was approved by Tony Blair, as Robin Cook made plain. It says the government 'should' make an early declaration, not that it must or, even better, that it will. So far it has not. The Queen's Speech contained two fistfuls of constitutional measures yet failed to present them as a coherent programme of democratic renewal. And White Papers on Freedom of Information can turn easily into white lies. (Harold Wilson lived by such techniques, while the country died by them.)

How have we managed to get this far? In a recent profile designed to expose and criticise the arguments of Charter 88, the *Daily Telegraph* proclaimed:

To conquer two of our three political parties is a remarkable achievement. But an even greater accomplishment is to take an abstract issue such as constitutional reform and make it the main fault-line in the coming election.

Meanwhile, the *Sunday Telegraph* argued that Charter 88 is the most successful think-tank of the 1990s and drew the comparison with CND. Both these attempts to measure the Charter's achievements misunderstand it. First, it was never purist like CND. From the beginning, it adopted a practical approach, arguing that because reforms are linked, to gain one would improve the prospect for gaining others. Thus partial success represents an overall gain not a compromise.

Second, the constitution is *not* an abstract issue. The regulation of power is tangible. Its rules are a means to an end. Everyone can understand this in any club or association in Britain. It is only our unwritten constitution that is remote from people's lives and - deliberately - abstracted. The belief that we should enjoy liberty, restrain the state, have equal votes and exercise local influence is widespread. I would not like to be the politician who tries to take away such powers once they are written down.

The Charter's success has not been due either to confounding intellectualism or CND-style demandism. Instead, it did not over-reach itself like most new organisations. It was genuinely cross-party yet did not split, as do most initiatives from the left. Nor, perhaps most important of all, did it become boring like most calls for reform. The basic demands have remained unchanged. But Charter 88 set out an inventive programme that explored the constitutional connections. Writers and playwrights, critics and economists, feminists and republicans, lawyers and trade unionists were all involved. It thereby became a reference point in our constitutional culture.

We thought we did not have a constitutional culture in England. Now we have. This is the source of the Charter's achievement. Mrs Thatcher challenged those who opposed her to stand up for themselves. The old Labour Party, co-responsible for consensus government, was too deep in Establishment routines to respond. Charter 88 did so, and it is to the credit of New Labour that, having heard the arguments, it has begun to embrace the cause.

We are still told that Labour leaders will shun reform in government. That no one who has worked to gain power will give it away. That Labour's initial, pusillanimous, response on Freedom of Information is the defining one. That the enjoyment of Britain's centralised parliamentary sovereignty will seduce its leaders as they see their reflections surrounded by the halo of authority. If this proves true it would be tragic. Should they fall in love with themselves in great office, the leaders of New Labour will pay the penalty of Narcissus. But for such enchantment to work in politics the spectators too have to be spellbound. The election shows the spell is broken. A constitutional revolution is on its way.

Northern Ireland, the Union and New Labour

Mary J Hickman

New Labour, new priorities?

On assuming power Tony Blair did the following in Northern Ireland: confirmed Mo Mowlam as Secretary of State, consulted with the leaders of what are referred to as the constitutional parties, visited Northern Ireland in record time and made a major speech which apparently held out something to both nationalists and unionists. This level of high-profile activity regarding Northern Ireland is unprecedented in the early life of a British administration; it is also notable in that it was not prompted by an immediate violent incident or a political threat from any of the many politically engaged groupings in Northern Ireland. The intention was obviously to recreate some of the momentum, and anticipation of a process for achieving peace, which the two ceasefires of 1994 generated.

Seemingly, therefore, Blair was immediately making good on one of his promises concerning Northern Ireland, which was that the peace process would not slip down the political agenda. This is important for a number of reasons. New Labour won a famous victory in May; their mandate to act across broad areas of civil society in order to change the priorities, policies and procedures by which people are governed is unquestioned, and the largest opposition party is greatly reduced in size and in disarray. This position of strong political authority affords an opportunity to tackle the complexities of a peace process in Northern Ireland without being 'in hock' to any one political party, and with the benefit of having a general mandate to bring about progressive social and political change (reinforced by significant votes cast for the Liberal Democrats and the Scottish National Party, both of whom advocate constitutional as well as social change). Because of the time undoubtedly required to reach agreement about the direction of change it is therefore of the first consequence that Northern Ireland has been placed high on the new administration's agenda early in its (first) term of government.

The high priority accorded to Northern Ireland is also important because of the significance of what is happening there. Northern Ireland is usually considered completely peripheral to other pressing political concerns in Britain. This is despite the high level of military engagement and despite the size of the subvention (the gap between tax revenue produced in Northern Ireland, and the cost of public provision, including the cost of the security forces, currently estimated at £3 billion per annum). The isolation and marginalisation of Northern Ireland has resulted from deliberate policies of both the British and Irish governments. In addition, the advocacy and use of violence by a variety of the political forces in Northern Ireland, and the dominance of cleavages informed by ethnicity, religion and nationality are deemed to set it as 'a place apart'.

The issues at stake in Northern Ireland do have a wider relevance for the United Kingdom as a whole. The successful insulation of Northern Ireland from the wider polity contributes to the seemingly incomprehensible use of extreme political tactics by different groupings in Northern Ireland. I want to discuss these issues of wider relevance, the dangers of marginalisation and the system of relationships within which Northern Ireland is placed.

New Labour, new policy on Northern Ireland?

Within three months of being elected leader of the party, and within days of the IRA ceasefire in August 1994, Tony Blair was signalling changes in the Labour Party's policy on Northern Ireland. The Anglo-Irish Agreement, and especially, the Downing Street Declaration, had in his view overtaken the historical position of all the main British parties in relation to Northern Ireland. These agreements, he stated, had enshrined British neutrality, in that the Tories had moved from a prescriptively unionist view that Northern Ireland should always remain within the United Kingdom, and the Labour Party had moved to a position of emphasising that it is up to the majority of people in Northern Ireland to determine their future. The principle of self-determination is cited by Blair as being crucial, and as meaning that the British government should not be persuaders for one policy or another (*Independent* 3.9.94). The Labour Party conference the following month, October 1994, agreed a new policy, which stated that Labour would 'seek to facilitate and encourage a balanced constitutional settlement leading to an agreement which will have the support of both traditions in Ireland'.

Three years later, two weeks after becoming Prime Minister, Blair gave a speech in Northern Ireland that appeared to signal further shifts in emphasis in Labour's policy. He reiterated all the above principles and gave a significant level of explicit support for the Union. This affirmation of the Union in the context of Northern Ireland is a further departure from Labour policy of the 1980s. He also announced that Northern Ireland Office officials would meet with Sinn Fein representatives to assess the likelihood of an IRA ceasefire. This was a departure from the previous government's policy of no contacts with Sinn Fein in the absence of a ceasefire, a policy which both Blair and Mo Mowlam had fully supported.

Blair's speech tried to deal with the fears of the Unionists that any concessions on an all-Ireland dimension beyond what already exists in the loathed Anglo-Irish Agreement would be a slippery slope to a united Ireland. Hence the strong statement on Northern Ireland's place in the Union; this appeared to satisfy David Trimble but would not necessarily have been reassuring to all Unionists, couched as it still was within what they view as the nationalist discourse of self-determination. Nationalist fears, that devolved government in Northern Ireland, unless backed at a minimum by significant power sharing and by a tangible Irish dimension (usually envisaged as cross-border institutions), would bring the return of a Stormont-type regime, were less wholeheartedly allayed. Blair's commitment is to sensible arrangements for co-operation with the Republic of Ireland, practical and institutional, which will be significant not only on the ground but also politically for the nationalist community. However, 'If such arrangements were really threatening to Unionists, we would not negotiate them.'

Blair has built his reputation since becoming leader of the Labour Party on projecting himself as a politician who communicates without artifice. We must therefore take this commitment to the Union and Northern Ireland's place in it at face value and not just as a device to keep the Unionists in talks. This strong message in favour of the Union is, of course, unsurprising from a Labour leader. Labour's constituency during the Thatcher years was largely based outside the South East and other parts of Middle England. This had implications for its policy towards the union. The significance of the general election in May was that at the same time as the Tories were wiped out in Scotland and Wales, Labour managed substantial success in Middle England.

For some time the Labour strongholds have been the metropolitan areas in England, and Scotland and Wales, and their proportion of the vote had been far greater in the latter pair than in the former. But Blair's crusade has been about reversing the marginality of Old Labour's role of bringing in the inner cities and the 'Celtic periphery' to the Union. In his speeches for a number of years he has emphasised not only 'one nation' but 'our nation'. The rationale for this campaign was that it represented the only means of gaining office, and it acknowledged the power of the expanding middle-classes in (southern) England. A discourse of the nation has thus inflected the centrist appeal of New Labour, and the nation Blair speaks of seems to be co-terminous with the Union.

Labour's aim is to keep the Union intact, and the proposals for devolution are its means to this end. The intention is to set up a Scottish parliament to handle Scotland's internal affairs such as education, health, local government, economic development and agriculture. Macro-economic policy, foreign affairs and social security would be left to Westminster. In Wales the intention is to establish a national assembly and in England regional councils. Blair has made it quite clear that Labour is not proposing a federation; thus, in Scotland the proposal is to devolve specific powers now handled by the Scottish office to a Scottish parliament. In this way the administrative devolution which already exists is being extended to 'proper political devolution' (*Guardian* 2.10.95). Proper political devolution fits into the decentralising, returning power closer to the people, rationale of new Labour rather than into any project for changing the fundamental basis of the Union. This was revealed during the election campaign when Blair likened the proposed Scottish parliament to an English parish council and stated that 'sovereignty rests with me as an English MP' (*Guardian* 7.4.97).

Labour's Scottish policy is projected as how in a New Britain the Union can be maintained, and it is also designed to head off the undoubted electoral threat that the SNP has been perceived to offer Labour in one of their three core areas of electoral strength. Landslides like May 1997 are not going to happen repeatedly.

When speaking about Northern Ireland after the election Blair articulated exactly what significance he attaches to the Union and the type of Union he visualises:

> The Union binds the four parts of the United Kingdom together. I believe in the United Kingdom. I value the Union.
>
> I want to see a Union which reflects and accommodates diversity. I am against a rigid, centralised approach. That is the surest way to weaken the Union. The Proposals this government are making for Scotland and Wales and for the English regions are destined to bring Government closer to the people. That will renew and strengthen the Union. I support this approach for Northern Ireland too, with some form of devolution and cross-border arrangements which acknowledge the importance of relationships in the island of Ireland. This is what the negotiations are about. We must of course devise arrangements which match the particular circumstances of Northern Ireland. Domination by one tradition or another is unacceptable (The Prime Minister, speaking at the Royal Ulster Agricultural Show, 16 May 1997).

Nothing could appear more reasonable than a Union that combines the accommodation of diversity and the decentralisation of power. In many ways, however, this presentation of the Union is not only remarkably similar to past invocations on the subject; it also appears in accord with recent Conservative thinking on the Union, apart from the commitment to devolution (see *Strengthening the United Kingdom*, Report of the Conservative Political Centre, 1996). It is over means rather than ends that the two parties differ on this matter.

New Unionism and debates on citizenship in Britain

The outright opposition of Unionists to the involvement of the Republic of Ireland in the affairs of Northern Ireland, effectively inaugurated by the Anglo-Irish Agreement in 1985, has led to two major developments in Unionism in Northern Ireland. Some Unionists have conceded the necessity of accepting power-sharing as part of devolved government, in order to stave off any further changes; but others have reformulated Unionism, and argue for full integration into the United Kingdom on the basis of equal citizenship rights with other UK citizens. In particular, this is a call for for full administrative, legislative and electoral integration, and would involve enabling citizens in Northern Ireland to vote for all British political parties as a means of foregrounding a left-right politics. For these Unionists the reformulation includes an acknowledgement that the old Stormont regime did disadvantage Catholics.

I want to examine this second perspective in some detail, because it is the preference of a large number of Unionists, and is also represented within the Labour Party in the shape of Democracy Now. This new Unionism is interesting because it explicitly rejects the notion that the crisis in Northern Ireland is about two competing national or ethnic identities. Instead the conflict is posited as between Irish nationalism and allegiance to the British state. Unionism in this account is concerned with issues of rights and citizenship, and distinguishes, unlike in its view Irish nationalism, between culture and political allegiance. It is advocating a political allegiance - that is, to the British state - the nature of which allows one to express whatever cultural values or identities one wishes. This is based on the premise that there is no British nation, there are only British citizens, so loyalty is to the idea of the Union: a willing communion of people united not by creed, colour or ethnicity but by recognition of the authority of that Union.[1]

These new Unionists (who encompass many young middle-class people) do not therefore see devolution as the solution. Instead they argue that integration is the way to provide equal opportunities for Catholics in Northern Ireland and equal opportunities for 'Ulster Catholics and

---

1. A. Aughey, *Under Siege: Ulster Unionism and the Anglo-Irish Agreement*, Blackstaff Press, Belfast 1989.

Protestants' in the United Kingdom. The new Unionism thus speaks directly to debates about equal opportunities and minorities in British society. The arguments of political theorists like Bhikhu Parekh are cited favourably and utilised to strengthen the argument for integration. Parekh has written about national identity in order to critique the right in Britain, and its notions of British stock which exclude West Indians and Asians. Parekh cites approvingly modern Europe's invention of a form of the state whose job it is to provide a framework of authority and a body of laws within which individuals and groups are at liberty to live the way they want. In his view, the more mature or developed a state the more it tolerates and welcomes religious, moral and cultural diversity, and the greater is its capacity to live with and develop unity out of religious, moral, cultural and ethnic diversity. Thus, to maintain that the unity of Britain must be based on the uniformity of the British nation, as the right does, is to imply that it is an immature and unsophisticated polity, and ignores British history.[2]

This universalist view of the state, denuded of all national and ethnic particularisms chimes well with the new Unionism in Northern Ireland, and enables them to make connections on the left of the political spectrum in Britain, something of a contrast to the Ulster Unionist Party's embrace of Enoch Powell in the 1970s. However, it is worth noting two aspects in particular of Parekh's argument. First, he specifically cites the assimilative capacity of British society, arguing that in Britain 'once the Huguenots, the Irish and the Jews settled down, they were soon second to none in their loyalty to the country'. All have been absorbed and 'now form part of the British stock ... In short, the British stock has been and is constantly expanding, and its evolutionary process cannot be arbitrarily ended or its boundaries closed at a convenient point in history'. Second, what Parekh seems to be offering the right, within his rather Whiggish model of state development, is a new version of superiority (that of being a mature polity) in order to attract them from the old one.

There are two problems here. First, a riposte to the right that remains on the territory of arguing about what really constitutes 'British stock' is a weak argument, as it gives credence to the racialised conceptual apparatus that they

---

2. B. Parekh, 'The New Right and the Politics of Nationhood', in G. Cohen *et al* (eds), *The New Right*, Runnymede Trust, London 1986.

employ to generate the legitimacy of their views. Second, no evidence is offered to substantiate either that the unity of the British state 'lies in its form, not in any substantive identity of race or unity of beliefs', or the proposition that the Irish and Jews have been unproblematically absorbed into 'British stock', and that their second generations are indistinguishable from the indigenous population in their loyalties and affections.

Claims about the constitution, and about the success of the Union, are integral aspects of what underpins notions of the superiority of being British. The ability of the British state to contain national differences and allow for their distinctive cultural and religious institutions has always been lauded as both its strength and its claim to be a crucible of the rule of law and personal liberty, and as such a model for others. This defence of the Union, which is put by people across the range of the left-right spectrum in Britain, is historically directly related to David Hume's thesis that the defining superiority of the English/British lies in the inter-breeding of different peoples and cultures which has taken place on this island. Hume argued specifically that this demonstrated the superiority of the British/English compared with the Irish, who were inferior in part because of their isolated in-breeding and because they had never experienced the Roman invasion from which 'all the Western world derived its civility'.

It is true that an individual does not have to feel an identification with the state in which she resides in order to recognise its legitimacy, but the reality is that a majority of people in Britain do invest some cultural substance into their notion of being British, as surveys even in Scotland and Wales show is the case. This is not because of the coincidence of their ethnicity with the state, but because the state project itself was nationalised, through the primary institutions of the school, the churches and the military. In this way the state actively intervened to construct political subjects and foster national consciousness. This national project has been contested from a number of directions, especially since the 1960s, but there is little evidence that it has ceased to have legitimacy for a majority in the United Kingdom - hence Blair's campaign and its use of the Union Jack flag and a bulldog.

Much has been written of the role of empire in this nationalisation project, especially on the nineteenth century. Rather less frequently is reference made to the role of Ireland, and this is due in part to the presence of all the island of

Ireland in the Union between 1801 and 1922. Ireland is, therefore, complicated for these discussions, evoking as it does both the domestic arena and the colonial arena. Consequently, Ireland has frequently been left out of analyses of the British state and Britishness.[3] In fact, the 1801 Act of Union and the 1829 Catholic Emancipation Act did not so much resolve the issue of the place of Irish Catholics in the Union as prompt a fierce debate about the Protestant Constitution, and raise fundamental questions about English/British national identity.

For example, in Parekh's schema Irish migrants and their descendants have been easily absorbed in Britain. But the absorption of the Irish in Britain (to the extent it has happened) is the result of specific incorporating strategies of the British state and the English and Scottish Catholic Churches. These strategies were initiated in the nineteenth century, and directed towards the denationalisation of the Irish when they were the only large settlement of labour migrants in British cities. For example, educational policies were a key component of the response to Irish migrants. The origin of state funding for Catholic schools in Britain lies not in a universalistic inspired extension of rights but in the wish to segregate Irish Catholic children from other working-class children. These strategies were successful in so far as they produced a low public profile for the majority of the Irish in Britain, and this is often misinterpreted as assimilation.[4]

Some Unionists cite as a reason to favour the Union that Irish Catholics who have chosen to live in Great Britain experience no oppression, nor do they suffer any social or political disadvantage. This argument lacks conviction, because it takes formal legal frameworks to be synonymous with institutional practices, and the experiences of individual migrants. The problem is that universal ideas of equal political and civil rights have not always been accompanied by social justice and equality. For example, in June 1997 the Commission for Racial Equality published a report on discrimination and the Irish community in Britain which raises question marks over the reported unproblematic assimilation of the Irish in Britain. And arguments that Catholics

---

3. See, for example, the rather spurious argument provided by Linda Colley for excluding Ireland from her analysis in *Britons: Forging the Nation*, Yale University Press, 1992.
4. M. J. Hickman, *Religion, Class and Identity. The state, the Catholic Church and the education of the Irish in Britain*, Avebury Press, Aldershot 1995.

have no disadvantage in Britain do not necessarily hold water for Scotland; and a constitutional settlement remains in place for the United Kingdom which excludes Catholics. This context suggests that a shortcoming of the new Unionism may be its refusal or inability to recognise an interrelationship between citizenship and cultural identities.[5]

Britishness and the Union

There is an ethnic particularity to Britishness. Not only does Britishness carry a conviction of its own superiority, which can be the basis of an ethnicising impulse; its English core has not been entirely eradicated, for example in the acceptance of an English dominated constitutional settlement. In addition, there still remains a residual secularised-Protestant identity as an element to Britishness. This explains why, although Catholics may be seen as having crossed the borderline into respectability, English Catholics are still more acceptable than Irish Catholics, and manifestations of anti-Catholicism are fairly commonplace in Scotland, and elsewhere are by no means unknown.

Britishness is an all-encompassing identity, and only allows certain options for expressions of belonging outside of being British. Primarily, it recognises the existence of other national identities, but these are positioned as subnational identities and as such are not hyphenated with Britishness, because the latter overarches them, the symbol of this being the Westminster parliament. The legitimacy of this distinction, and the material resources it has delivered, is what has partly sustained the Union. In a similar way, the ethnic identifications of those who are visibly different (the ethnic identifications of everyone else are subsumed under the category 'White') are categorised as those of ethnic minorities; their subordinate position in the hierarchy is securely located and it has delivered limited earmarked resources.

For all these and other reasons national and ethnic struggles have been the form in which challenges to the British state have manifested themselves. Challenges have taken this form not solely because they are the expression of what are often viewed as atavistic national and ethnic agendas. Making and maintaining these national and ethnic distinctions has been part of the British

---

5. For further discussion of the new Unionism see N. Porter, *Rethinking Unionism*, Blackstaff Press, Belfast 1996..

state project. They have constituted part of how the state has managed, amongst other things: the economy, and class and regional differences. These distinctions can therefore be the basis of practices of both inclusion and exclusion, and the same group can be excluded or included at different junctures. Simultaneously, the rhetoric of the nation, that is, the 'we' of being British, glosses over or ignores these divisions.

U nlike Parekh, many black Britons have recognised the close intertwining of citizenship and cultural identity in Britain, and have pointed out forcefully that their presence in the metropole as full and equal citizens requires a reformulation of Britishness which can encompass their identities as both British and in terms of specific different ethnicities. Many argue that membership of a specific ethnic community has to be accorded a greater political importance than has previously been the case, but that this should exist in parallel with a meaningful membership of the body politic which brings citizens together regardless of ethnic group membership. Pressure therefore exists from a number of quarters for fundamental changes in the Union.

The particularity of an Irish (Catholic) national identity has been one that the British state has had specific difficulties in accommodating. This was because the ethnic particularity of Britishness could not encompass Irish identity as a sub-national identity in the same way as it could those of Scotland and Wales, in part because of the centrality of Protestantism for Britishness. Highly significant also were the different economic relationships, and the different bases of the Unions, forged by England with each of the other countries. Catholic Ireland historically has been as important as Catholic France for forging a sense of Britishness amongst the disparate populations of England, Wales and Scotland.

U nionism as currently espoused in Northern Ireland and Britain remains, when deconstructed, in the grip of the binary opposition of the British and Irish spheres, with the British taken for granted as more progressive than the Irish. The implicit comparison is always between a civic nation state (the United Kingdom) and an ethno-cultural nation state (Republic of Ireland). In reality tension exists between civic and ethno-cultural nationalisms in the polity of both states. Casting the Republic of Ireland as backward in the sense of being parochical, politically illiberal, religiously superstitious and nationalist in a retrograde way is a habit not only of Unionists in Northern Ireland but of many, although not all, political and media commentators in Britain. This demonstrates that the Othering of 'Catholic Ireland' is still a marker for the superiority of being British.

The British state is not post-imperial, post-ethnic or post-Protestant. There is sufficient contestation in a variety of domains to warrant a description of it as going through a process that may result in those adjectives being appropriate. Significantly, it is the contestations taking place in England (and the exit from Hong Kong) which are given greatest weight: the agenda for change is still set from the centre, Scottish and Welsh concerns are viewed as parochial, and nationalism as manifest in Northern Ireland is viewed as an aberration.[6] The Republic of Ireland is not post-Catholic or post-ethno-national; it too, however, is going through processes which are responding to membership of the European Union, globalisation, and to the accommodation of a variety of ways of being Irish, which means that it has experienced a significant degree of social liberalisation and economic progress in recent years.

The Union as currently constituted cannot provide the framework for settling Catholic grievances and the conditions for peace and reconciliation. The continuance in place of the 1688 constitution, the evidence of racism and discrimination directed towards Irish people because of their ethnicity, and the so far unreformulated notions of Britishness, are all major obstacles in the path of integration as a means of creating the conditions for peace and reconciliation in Northern Ireland. Nor is a united Ireland the means of achieving peace and reconciliation at the current time. It would take a very different Northern Ireland from the one that exists at the moment to 'consent' to unification. Significantly, neither government supports integrationist proposals since integration would destroy the careful insulation of events in Northern Ireland from the political life of both states. That is the logic behind the devolution proposals in the Framework Document.

Northern Ireland and the Union

Part of the dilemma in Northern Ireland is to discover a state form which could accommodate the republican challenge, which has never been based solely on

---

6. For this and a number of other points I am indebted to J. Ruane and J. Todd , *The Dynamics of Conflict in Northern Ireland: Power, Conflict and Emancipation*, Cambridge University Press, Cambridge 1996.

the claims of ethnic nationalism, but has involved a critique of the legitimacy of the state. The British state, in the form of successive governments, tolerated the institutionalised disadvantaging of Catholics by the Stormont regime for fifty years, as long as events in Northern Ireland did not impinge on the rest of the citizenry of the United Kingdom. The basis of the original civil rights campaign in Northern Ireland in 1967-8 was a claim for full citizenship status for all persons under equal protection of the law: 'British rights for British citizens'. This led, although not irrevocably, to the longest-running armed challenge to a state in western Europe since 1945.

Is devolution backed by power-sharing a framework for dealing with this challenge, and the fears of the Unionists? One major argument against devolution in general is that it is a measure that heightens national differences. The Tory view is that in Scotland devolution will lead to the breakup of the Union - their lack of 'selfish economic and strategic interest' in Northern Ireland does not extend to Scotland. On the other hand, as stated earlier, Labour think devolution will save the Union, but the party's proposals for Scotland and Wales appear to reinforce the hierarchical boundaries of difference which are part of the Union. The argument against devolution in Northern Ireland is that it will range itself along the nationalist/unionist faultline and consequently rekindle the conflict. The checks and balances built into the political institutions proposed in the Framework Document might well cement nationalist and unionist identities and differences, with little chance for the formation of cross-community alliances. This would be all the more likely to happen if this structure was imposed on a situation in which little else had changed.

Responding to this situation some groupings have supported a 'Europe of the Regions', and others suggest a British Archipelago in which power is devolved to highly localised areas, combined with the establishment of an equivalent of the inter-governmental 'Nordic Council' which brings together Denmark, Finland, Iceland, Norway, Sweden, the Faroe Islands, Greenland and the Åland Islands. Whatever merits these latter two proposals have, both of these suggestions are long term. It seems more urgent to address the communal polarisation as it exists today. At one level, nationalists can afford to wait - the demography is going their way, the first nationalist mayor of Belfast has been elected; but this is not an adequate response to a Unionist sense of siege, nor will it deal more immediately with the remaining Catholic sense of unredressed grievances.

So what of new Labour's Northern Ireland policy? It might be argued that Blair's conception of the Union owes nothing to the Old Britain aggrandising notions discussed above. That it is securely rooted within the enlightenment project Blair has in mind for the New Britain. Blair is, in many ways, tackling the problem of articulating a post-imperial role for the United Kingdom. However, he is relatively silent about many of the aspects of the reconstruction that would be necessary if the legacies of empire - which still exercise significant power over attitudes, notions of national identity and narrative - and national pride in Britain are to be excised.

Hugo Young has pointed out that Blair's notion of 'one of us' is all-embracing, and he seeks to absorb 'everyone who matters' to his project for Britain (*Guardian* 27.5.97). This inclusivity is welcome after the past eighteen years, but could in fact be quite alarming, because it seems to be based on denying difference, rather than on recognising and accommodating difference, in its concept of the nation. The enlightenment project is an attractive one, based as it is on a concept of universal citizenship based on the equal moral worth of all persons; but it has, as many critiques have highlighted, to be treated with caution. This is because citizenship for all implies that citizenship transcends particularity and differences; but the idea that citizenship is the same for all translates in practice to the requirement that all citizens be the same.

Iris Marion Young argues that a democratic public should provide mechanisms for the effective representation and recognition of the distinct voices, and perspectives, of those of its constituent groups who are disadvantaged or historically have been excluded. To ensure equality, it is not enough to enable excluded groups to assimilate and live by the norms of dominant groups. They should be able to have their 'difference' recognised and supported in both the public and private spheres. Providing for group representation in a forum which necessitates that people encounter the opinions of others who do not have the same perspectives is part of the process. In a variety of arenas decisions can then be reached on claims for social justice. This process has to be achieved at many levels in a society, not just in formal political institutions.[7]

The universalist would obviously find a contradiction in asserting both that

7. I. M. Young, 'Polity and Group Difference: a Critique of the Ideal of Universal Citizenship', *Ethics*, Vol.99, No.2, 1989.

formerly segregated groups have a right to inclusion and that these groups have a right to different treatment. There is no contradiction, however, if attending to difference is necessary in order to make participation and inclusion possible. The politics of the Northern Ireland Women's Coalition have demonstrated this. Their raft of candidates for the Forum election in May 1996 was rigorously scrutinised to ensure that it was cross-class, cross-region and cross-sector, as they were determined not to reproduce the existing class and political relations of the mainstream political parties. In addition, their insistence, after much debate, on three principles - Inclusion, Equity and Human Rights - was controversial, because it essentially argued for the inclusion of Sinn Fein and the Loyalist parties in the peace process, irrespective of ceasefires being put in place or maintained, and adhered to the perception that everyone needed to be in dialogue.

Two other contexts in which universalist principles are counter-productive are worth considering. It has recently been estimated that the systematic adoption of meritocratic principles for appointments to the RUC will mean that it will take fifty years to increase the proportion of Catholics who serve on the force from seven to twenty percent.[8] Without some affirmative action guidelines it is difficult to see how a demonstrably non-sectarian police force and mode of policing can be introduced in Northern Ireland. The only other alternative would be disbandment and the construction of a new police force. In relation to employment it is not enough to ensure that equal opportunity policies are in place and implemented so that Catholics and Protestants can apply and be considered for all jobs. Other measures may have to be taken to ensure both Protestants and Catholics are able to feel they can go after a job wherever there is a vacancy, rather than having to check first to see where it is located. It is not only state institutions that have to address these matters, employers, amongst others, have to consider the multi-various ways in which they could contribute to encouraging dialogue and a changing climate. This is not a process the Catholic or Protestant middle-classes should be able to insulate themselves from.

Many of Labour's policies, as articulated by Mo Mowlam, are designed to increase levels of trust on all sides. This is being attempted through a more pro-

---

8.   G. Ellison, 'Under Fire, *Fortnight*, No. 362, June 1997.

active strategy of confidence-raising measures than previously existed. The aim is even-handedness over a range of measures. The contrast in style with the previous Secretary of State, and indeed with the last Labour appointee to the post, Roy Mason, can but be positive. Not the least aspect of the change is the fact that Mowlam is a woman and has already given indications of a commitment to dialogue. However, this is a strategy with many risks, as each measure will have appeal, usually, to one community rather than the other. In the months ahead there will be many tests of Labour policies, and whether they are informed by a workable strategy.

A workable strategy is not one that continues to insulate the issues at stake in Northern Ireland from the rest of British political life. Nor is it one that continues to respond and judge events in Northern Ireland with no acknowledgement of how British priorities and policies impact on the situation. Without a comprehensive appraisal of the situation in Northern Ireland, in the context of the whole system of relationships that exists between the two states, the fine seeming principles of consent, the wish of the majority and gaining the commitment of both communities will be empty words. As things stand at the moment, consent can easily mean a veto for the majority community: the Unionists. If a majority was arrived at which involved the two largest political parties, the UUP and SDLP, there could be some demonstration of cross-community support (it should be noted, however, that twenty five years of attempts have not brought that particular agreement about). Neither of these parties, however, fully represents the working-class communities without whom there will be no long term settlement of the issues.

Although the resort to and the level of violence in Northern Ireland is regularly condemned, nearly three decades of condemnations has done little to mitigate the ferocity of incidents perpetrated by all sides. The pathologisation of the paramilitaries is not necessarily helpful either. Frequently the 'ordinary, decent people' of Northern Ireland are contrasted with the 'men of violence' and exhorted to put pressure on them to cease (see, for example, *New Statesman* 23.2.96). In the past the extent of real, albeit often very reluctant, support for paramilitary actions in working-class communities has never been sufficiently acknowledged. The rise in Sinn Fein's vote in three successive elections between May 1996 and May 1997 is a vote for peace, as Sinn Fein has consistently claimed, but it is also a demonstration of community support which refutes pathologising paradigms. Rising support for the PUP and the UDP in the May 1997 local government elections can be similarly explained.

These political forces are seen as the most extreme, but have given rise to some of the most significant political shifts in Northern Ireland. The importance of both republican and loyalist prisoners in urging different strategies and reflecting on ways forward for Northern Ireland is often underestimated. Flexibility is demonstrated in other ways. For example, there is working-class support for full integration into the United Kingdom; in the Progressive Unionist Party, it would probably be viewed as the first preference. However, they acknowledge that full integration is unrealistic given the aspirations of the nationalist community. This, from their perspective, is a considerable contribution to the prospects for negotiations.[9]

Sinn Fein remain the most demonised of political forces despite being the third largest political party. Relatively little credit is given, in public, to the political leadership of Sinn Fein for developing a strategy for making the party politically relevant in the long term. Their obvious willingness to participate in negotiations if the conditions their own supporters want are fulfilled is a recognition that only a negotiated political settlement that commands cross-community support will bring about peace. Differences exist amongst republicans on this, but a majority have supported Sinn Fein's strategy for peace, urged on by critical Irish-American support. To cast them in terms of just seeking a substitute 'Green majoritarianism' underestimates the debate underway within the movement.

An unequivocal IRA ceasefire remains a pre-condition for Sinn Fein's entry into the all-party talks. If and when it occurs their entry into talks should on the basis of their electoral mandate. If one considers the situation, as I write in early summer 1997, of the Joint Loyalist Military Command ceasefire, one could argue that it holds in words (that is, there is an absence of words to say it is over) but not in deeds. The Chief Constable of the RUC on a number of recent occasions has expressed the view that it is disintegrating if not over. The PUP and UDP, however, remain in the talks. So they should be, but so should the application of criteria for entry be even-handed.

---

9. D. Ervine, *Northern Ireland What Next?*, Conference Report, University of North London Press, London 1995.

Instead of acting together to insulate Northern Ireland from affecting their respective 'body politics', the British and Irish governments may have to take further steps to show leadership that might advance the commitments they made in the Downing Street Declaration. In his May 1997 speech Blair said that if the Irish government altered the Irish constitution and removed the territorial claim to the whole of the island of Ireland this would go a long way towards alleviating Unionist fears about the slide into a united Ireland. There can be no doubt that this would be a very significant step towards the creation of the conditions for peace and reconciliation (although this is unlikely to gain the necessary support outside of the context of a political settlement). However, there was nothing in the speech about the necessity of equivalent moves by the British government.

What could these equivalent moves be? This article has been a statement of the case for a reformulation of Britishness, for change in the Union, for the necessity of ensuring that the constitutional reforms new Labour undertakes are wide-ranging (including the separation of church and state and the equal representation of all ethnicities), and for recognising that on current evidence reforming the state in Northern Ireland so that meritocratic, universalist practices reign will not be enough. The political settlement currently being striven for cannot be one that incubates conflict again in a few years time. Reconciling nationality and equality is a fundamental issue of democracy as we head towards the Millennium; this is why what happens in Northern Ireland is so important for the polities of both the United Kingdom and the Republic of Ireland.

The Union as currently constituted carries a national culture and public symbols which are exclusionary of many of its citizens both in Britain and Northern Ireland. Cross-border institutions and internal arrangements which alter both the symbols of the nation state and guarantee the voice of the minority are an essential minimum in Northern Ireland. Unionists fear their absorption by an assimilating Irish nationalism and have the right to say 'no' to any arrangements that might presage that eventuality. However, the ostensible cultural pluralism of the United Kingdom, predicated as it is on a hierarchical system of relationships, has no necessary legitimacy for a sizeable minority in Northern Ireland; and all sides, not just *both* sides, have to develop a language to address both these problematics in negotiation.

Tackling regional inequality in Europe

Ash Amin

The growing regional divide

Labour's historic victory provides the government with a real opportunity to tackle the regional economic inequalities which have steadily grown over the last two decades. Market forces, combined with highly selective centralising policies introduced by the Conservatives, have worked to the advantage of the fittest and most powerful economic interests, located in the most prosperous regions. The less favoured regions, beyond the Greater South East, which include both the declining industrial or urban areas and the lagging rural or semi-rural areas, have had to face the full onslaught of reduced state intervention, out-migration of resources, exposure to more competitive regions, and costly campaigns to attract relatively scarce investment.

Regional economic polarisation is not unique to the UK, but part of a wider trend in Europe. Measures of productivity (GDP per head) and unemployment are among the most commonly used indicators of regional economic dynamism. Figure 1 shows that since the early 1980s, while inter-state productivity differences have tended to converge, inter-regional disparities remain very high, with little sign of convergence. Figure 2 shows that regional disparities in unemployment have steadily grown since the mid 1970s, and remain higher than national differences. Thus, the gap between the least and most prosperous regions, as shown in Table 1, remains extremely high, with some alarming increases in the unemployment gap over the last decade. By the admission of the European Commission itself, the power-houses of the new European economy are the major cities and 'islands' of technological innovation which lie in the broad arc of

53

Regional disparities in income, productivity and unemployment in the European Union, 1983 and 1993						
	GDP per head (PPS, EUR15 = 100)		GDP per person employed (EUR15 = 100)		Unemployment (% labour force)	
	1983	1993	1983	1993	1983	1993
Between Member States						
Best-off	134.8	160.1	124.2	124.3	3.3	2.3
Worst-off	55.1	63.2	51.3	58.6	17.4	22.3
Best-off / Worst-off [1]	2.4	2.5	2.4	2.1	5.3	9.7
Standard Deviation	17.2	12.8	13.5	14.4	3.1	4.6
Gini coefficient	*0.089*	*0.059*				
Between Regions						
Best-off	184.0	189.0	398.0	420.4	1.7	3.2
Worst-off	39.0	37.0	32.1	36.6	22.5	33.3
Best-off / Worst-off [1]	5.0	4.5	12.4	11.5	13.2	9.0
10 Best-off	154.0	158.0	146.0	156.0	3.8	3.9
10 Worst-off	44.0	48.0	49.4	48.6	19.4	26.4
10 Best-off / Worst-off [1]	3.2	3.1	3.0	3.2	5.1	6.8
25 Best-off	140.0	142.0	131.3	130.7	4.8	4.6
25 Worst-off	53.0	55.0	63.3	63.1	17.2	22.4
25 Best-off / Worst-off [1]	2.5	2.5	2.1	2.1	3.6	4.9
Standard Deviation	26.8	27.2	18.0	17.6	4.2	6.0
Gini coefficient	*0.149*	*0.153*				

Table 1　　[1] For unemployment, highest unemployment rate / lowest unemployment rate　　Source: CEC (1996) *First Cohesion Report*, European Commission, Brussels.

prosperity that sweeps south-eastwards from London to northern Italy, across the Netherlands, northern France, central Germany, and north-east Spain, leaving much of the UK, Ireland, North European industrial regions, and the southern Mediterranean out in the cold.

The present trend in Europe reverses the steady decrease in regional disparities during the golden years of economic expansion after 1960, when lucrative regional incentives and other forms of active state intervention succeeded in redirecting surplus investment and employment from the economic core to the periphery. Now, after nearly two decades of sluggish growth following the end of the post-war boom, and mounting ideological and practical scepticism against state economic intervention, the less favoured regions face the prospect of having to compete for relatively scarce economic opportunities in a world of intensified inter-regional competition.

Contemporary EU economic policy, largely inspired by neo-liberal values, is exacerbating the regional problem. EU competitiveness policies, which are designed to strengthen European companies in the face of competition from Japanese and

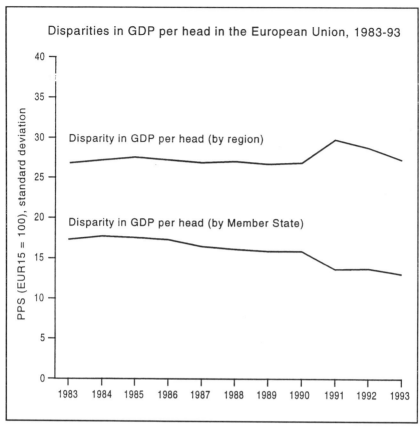

Disparities in GDP per head in the European Union, 1983-93

Figure 1

Source: CEC (1996) First Cohesion Report, *European Commission, Brussels.*

American companies, are serving to reinforce the hand of large firms and institutions of the core regions. For example, these regions have been the major beneficiaries of incentives provided under the EU's various technology programmes which support cross-border Research and Development. Similarly, EU Competition Policy scrutinises the anti-competitiveness effects of only the largest and most visible cross-border mergers and acquisitions, deliberately leaving untouched the vast majority (together with joint ventures and alliances), in order to encourage the formation of world-beating giant European corporations. This basic aim also lies behind the '1992' proposals, which sought to remove trade barriers, reduce national purchasing preferences, and harmonise standards across the member states, in the hope that the increased market opportunities would provide large firms with

55

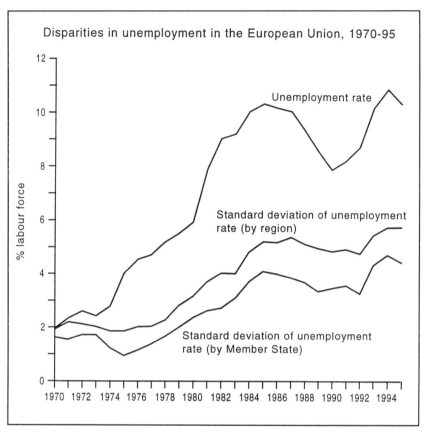

Figure 2

Source: CEC (1996) *First Cohesion Report*,
European Commission, Brussels.

sufficient scale economies. All these actions are conceding to the strengths of the core regions as sites of demand, skills, know-how, specialist infrastructure, services, and various other economies of agglomeration. For less favoured regions, the market-shock poses a serious threat, risking the cumulative pull of resources towards the expanding regions, together with the failure of local firms to survive the competition from firms benefiting from the externalities offered by the asset-rich regions.

The European Commission acknowledges the centralising risks associated with its economic policies. On offer as a corrective are its so-called cohesion policies, which include target funding for the less prosperous regions. EU regional policy has evolved from its original role, of providing direct incentives to target firms and sectors to locate in the regions, towards supporting indirect supply-side interventions serving to enhance regional economic competitiveness. The belief is that long-term success can only be secured through efforts to improve the quality of regional infrastructure - from the built environment and transport and communications, to education and training. Regions can then compete their way to prosperity, by attracting inward investment and nurturing their own entrepreneurs and small firms. In addition, within EU regional policy, the allocation of funds has become increasingly tied to the ability of a region to demonstrate its institutional capacity to develop, implement, and evaluate long-term, integrated development plans.

These lofty goals which have been set for the less favoured regions are likely to be achieved with great difficulty in a neo-liberal macroeconomic context that favours the strongest regions. There are at least three grounds for pessimism. First, with EU unemployment levels mounting to alarming heights (a record average of 11 per cent), it is clear that there is no economic expansion taking place in Europe. This diminishes the scope for any 'trickle-down' of growth to the less favoured regions as a consequence of any overheating in the core regions. Second, in financial terms, EU regional policy offers too little, spread too thinly: total expenditure amounts to less than 0.5 per cent of the Union's total GDP. In the mid 1970s, when the scale and intensity of regional disparities was less pronounced than now, the Commission's own calculations suggested the need for a minimum transfer of resources amounting to 5-7 per cent of EU total GDP in order significantly to reduce the regional divide. Third, in the present context of intensified inter-regional competition, and restricted financial transfers, it is a tall order indeed to expect the less favoured regions to unlock their competitive potential, and to such a degree as to secure self-regenerating growth.

Labour's challenge:
competitiveness through social cohesion

What lies at the heart of the policy dilemma in Europe is a failure to decide on whether cohesion - social and regional - should be seen as a source, or consequence, of economic competitiveness. Labour, with its commitment to regional devolution, the stakeholder economy, and social justice, and its desire to play a positive role in Europe, is in a strong position to champion the cause of prosperity *through* regional and social cohesion. Although the momentum for exploring the economic potential of society-building is growing in Europe, the idea that region-building too could lie at the centre of a new European Model, has gained less ground. Labour can really take the lead here, by developing its ideas on regional devolution beyond its present scope, to incorporate new thinking on the benefits offered by the 'social economy'.

During much of the post-war period, the continental European model of economic regulation - commonly known as the European Social Model - sought to achieve economic competitiveness through the regulated market, and social cohesion through the redistributive state. This model is being challenged by long-maturing structural changes which necessitate a new model of economic and political organisation. The changes include:

◆ A fiscal limit on macroeconomic expansion and welfare expenditure posed by the break-down of the post-war model of growth in which increases in productivity secured parallel increases in employment.

◆ Widening social polarisation and deepening social exclusion, partly as a consequence of the above, and not likely to be resolved simply through reintegration within the formal economic mainstream.

◆ New forms of economic competitiveness, drawing on learning and continual adaptation, worker involvement, market interaction through networks of association, and generally, the economics of trust and reciprocity.

◆ The rise of plural authority structures alongside the state and traditional corporatist structures (e.g. associations, NGOs, quangos, etc.), as well as a new distribution of authority and responsibility between the local, national and European state.

◆ The rise of new forms of politics alongside more traditional representative or corporatist models, drawing on grass-roots mobilisation, popular protest, issue campaigns and expedient alliances, and so on.

The result is that economic and political life has become increasingly heterogeneous and changeable, and, therefore, more difficult to manage and regulate through singular logics of governance such as market- or state-based allocation. One consequence of the ensuing crisis of traditional expectations from both the formal economy and the state is the opening-up of a third space of organisation that, at least potentially, might allow a reconnection of the economic and the social spheres in novel ways. Two significant aspects of this third space are, firstly, the social economy as a source of income and employment, and secondly, social participation as a source of governance.

The social economy

One observation that follows from the trends outlined above is that economic efficiency is increasingly a matter of mobilising social networks. Another is that the formal market economy is not likely to generate a satisfactory level of employment in Europe. Taken together, they suggest the need for a new European Social Model that explicitly recognises the value of social participation as a source of economic efficiency and reward.

From the first observation, it is clear from the experience of the most dynamic and innovative global corporations, as well as dynamic small-firm regions in Europe, that success in volatile international markets is predicated upon the ability to upgrade the quality of products and competencies, gain access to information, innovation and knowledge, and secure organisational flexibility, learning and adaptation. These are capabilities that draw upon continual training and skill upgrading, mobilisation of competencies throughout the organisation, cultures of mutuality and reciprocity, decision-making and governance through interaction, and links of long-term commitment between buyers and suppliers. They are part of a model of organisation that privileges the economics of association, rather than the economics of contract or hierarchy as traditionally theorised by the economic orthodoxy.

This model legitimates, on grounds of *efficiency*, the desirability of incorporating social participation and dialogue as an essential component of any European standard on economic competitiveness. Politically, it is important that Labour openly acknowledges this aspect of the socialised economy, because, among other things, it would give its current defence of basic worker rights on grounds of social justice considerable economic legitimacy.

Turning to the second observation, if there is any truth in the 'jobless growth' hypothesis which suggests that the competitive economy is not likely to guarantee a return to full employment, a new European Social Model will need to strengthen the so-called social economy or third sector as a legitimate source of gainful employment and social reintegration. Indeed, in recognition of this problem, the European Commission is now showing considerable policy interest in initiatives to combat social exclusion which simultaneously meet social welfare needs and provide jobs, training and entrepreneurship opportunities to the weakest and most marginalised social groups. Typically, an initiative might provide services in local markets for domestic services, housing, personal and domestic security, mobility and access, community health, consumer services, cultural activity, and environmental protection, with delivery mobilised through a variety of actors including voluntary and community organisations, NGOs, co-operatives, profit-making firms, and partnerships of one kind or another. In its most innovative guise, the idea is to generate a market for socially useful projects in such a way that both provision and access are decoupled from the ability of individuals to pay unaffordable prices.

The central policy point is that in a new European Social Model, the social economy ought to be considered as legitimate a strand of economic life as the market or the state. Clearly, in a country like the UK, devastated under the Conservatives by a profiteering economy and a shrinking welfare state, the social economy promises considerable scope for expansion. It should be embraced by Labour, but with due care given to prevent it from degenerating into a market for exploitative, poor quality, or underpaid work.

Participatory governance

Historically, the role of the state within the European Social Model has been to secure macroeconomic stability, protect sectors of strategic or general national interest, redistribute income, meet universal welfare needs, and protect individual and state security. This is a role that in part derives from a constructivist legacy of decision-making, built around a faith in the virtues of planning, universal provision, mass identification, and representative democracy. Neo-liberals have traditionally questioned this legacy through the dubious claim that the market is a better and fairer provider. But now, a more persuasive challenge - potentially an opportunity for 'filling in' society - is posed by the rise of the new collective forces outlined earlier, such as plural and decentralised authority structures, and new forms of political engagement. The new Europe will defy management based on the rules of hierarchy and a central authority.

The principal paradox now faced by a central authority such as the state is how to co-ordinate a social system of many self-regulating parts which, however, do not come together into a whole. This is a task for which routine government or the enactment plan is inadequate. Instead it requires a new kind of state - an *enabling strategic* state whose role is to provide overall vision, and collective responsibility through, for example, arbitration between plural decision-making bodies, provision for universal needs, and resources for those least able to provide for themselves. These are not simply technicalities concerning how best to achieve society-wide reach, but also matters of political choice and behaviour: implicit is an extension and deepening of egalitarian and participatory principles.

The real test is whether the forces of social democracy in Europe can, with confidence and conviction, develop and legitimate a new form of state practice, based around the above dimensions of democratic associationalism, to supplement the traditional commitment to representative politics and redistributive justice. This is not a light task, since it requires a radical break from any ingrained centralist or hierarchical culture. At one level this necessitates a shift in state behaviour towards recognition of the legitimacy of a heterogeneous and plural decision-making community, belief in policy formulation through recursive interaction and dialogue with others, commitment to open, accountable and transparent government, and, critically, preparation for playing the role of strategic guide, arbitrator and facilitator in public life. At another level, democratic associationalism requires an uncompromising belief in democratisation as a source of creativity, innovation and renewal in advanced modern societies. This means placing confidence in many of the taboos of contemporary neo-liberal thought, including the legitimacy of self-organisation and decentred decision-making, workplace democracy and social ownership, the empowerment of weaker, under-represented and minority sections of society, and generally, the politics of dialogue and contestation between knowledgeable communities as a source of social innovation.

The next step forward for social democracy, thus, includes the socialisation of the economy and the democratisation of democracy itself. Labour, with its claim to radical change, is well placed to take this step, to play a leading intellectual and practical role in forging a new European Social Model.

Making connections:
region-building in the new European social model

Labour should seek to incorporate the principles of the social economy within its plans for the regions, in order to overcome the regional deficiencies of contemporary EU economic policies. At present, its plans for regional devolution seem only marginally connected with its ideas on regional policy. Not only does this gap need closing, but, as I argue below, Labour desperately needs to broaden its understanding of what constitutes appropriate economic and political action at the local level.

Economies of association

If economic action in the less favoured regions stops at the expectations of EU regional policy, it will not achieve a great deal. The experience of some of the most dynamic economies in Europe shows that supply-side upgrading of a generic nature (e.g. advanced transport and communications systems, or provision of specialised training and skills), integrated regional development plans, and powerful unitary development agencies (as Labour currently proposes), though desirable, are not sufficient to secure regional economic competitiveness. Instead, in small nations such as Denmark, and successful regional economies such as Emilia Romagna, Baden Würtemberg and Catalonia, policy action is increasingly centred around supporting clusters of inter-related industries which have long enough roots in the region's skill- or capabilities-base to secure meaningful competitive advantage.

Firm-specific initiatives, such as small-firm development programmes, or incentives to attract inward investors, tend to be integrated within such cluster programmes, in order to build up a system of local inter-dependencies. Institutional support, in the form of technology transfer, training and education, access to producer services such as market intelligence, business innovation, and finance, tends to be provided at the level of sectoral specificity, so that help can be targeted to firms in specific clusters.

In addition, considerable policy attention is paid to building economies of association. This might include efforts to improve cultures of innovation within firms by encouraging social dialogue and negotiation, worker participation, and learning based on shared knowledge and information exchange. It might also include initiatives to encourage inter-firm exchange and reciprocity, through buyer-supplier linkage programmes, incentives for pooling of resources, joint-ventures, task specialisation, and so on. Finally, it almost certainly includes a considerable degree of contact between the seemingly myriad institutions which represent local economic interests in these regions, from trade associations, large and small-firm lobbies and producer services agencies, to trade unions, chambers of commerce, local authorities, regional development agencies, and other intermediate institutions such as the commercial media.

The regional economic policy implications are clear. Attention needs to be paid to developing institutional capacity and infrastructural support around sectoral networks of horizontal and vertical inter-dependency. Such a frame of action privileges the spread of capabilities, economic innovation through social interaction, and mutually reinforcing regional economic networks. Its logic is qualitatively different from the 'imperative' logic embedded in the policy discourse of unitary development agencies and integrated regional plans.

In frankness, the economic benefits of this 'interactive' approach, rooted in institution-building, are not guaranteed in the short term. It involves a process of slow and cumulative change, and it also risks derailment by vested economic interests which have long benefited from their hegemonic dominance in regions of scarce resources and under-developed institutional capacity. The power of these vested interests needs to be acknowledged, and if needs be, directly challenged.

Innovative local initiatives to combat social exclusion

For the reasons given earlier, growth through improvements in regional economic competitiveness is not likely to secure full employment, above all in these regions of high and structural unemployment. More direct action is required to combat unemployment, and other forms of local social exclusion such as deprivation of basic needs and services. What is essential, however, is that such action serves as a catalyst for building a social economy that is able to provide jobs and nurture skills, expertise, and capabilities among those involved in it. In other words, the battle against social exclusion needs to build outwards from the provision of welfare, towards building an intermediate economic sphere that serves to meet real social needs. This could be through support for a community group that employs school leavers to offer affordable housing to low-income groups, or a cooperative that focuses on the long-term unemployed to provide domestic care or transport access to the elderly.

Labour is clearly not opposed to these ideas, as illustrated by its welfare-to-work programme. There is a danger, however, that the government schemes will end up being too narrowly defined, owing to their reliance on the United States as a role model for getting the unemployed back into work. The much vaunted example is the use of welfare benefits for part-payment to unemployed youths placed on training programmes or short-term work experience in partly-subsidised firms. Much comment has been made on the enforced, short-term, and potentially exploitative risks associated with such 'workfare' schemes, but an added problem is the tendency to assume that the only available option is reintegration into the formal labour market, which increasingly is failing to deliver secure jobs.

Labour would do well to explore ways of expanding and supporting the local social economy, as have done governments in the Scandinavian countries, Germany, France, Belgium, Netherlands, Italy, and Ireland. The thrust of effort in these countries has been to provide subsidies and other forms of support (e.g. training, facilitative legislation, specialised services), through national programmes as well as local initiatives, to community-based economic development projects which draw in target excluded groups as providers or users of socially useful services.

In the course of our work for the European Commission to construct a UK-wide database of local initiatives to combat social exclusion, we are discovering the existence of a myriad of fledgling or precariously balanced intiatives, largely supported by the voluntary sector or non-profit organisations, whose long-term survival is constantly threatened by financial or credit insecurity. The government could help by strengthening the long-term financial security of these initiatives. In addition, other research is revealing that years of Tory exclusion and financial deprivation have forced the rise, in many parts of the country, of 'alternative' trading systems and innovative metrics of exchange as a coping mechanism. These include, for example, the non-monetary exchange of consumer and personal services (e.g. child-care, washing, car repairs) between individuals and families, calculated on the basis of time-equivalents, or community credit networks which pool income and might also exchange cash for services. Both these illustrations reveal unorthodox problems which not only badly need policy attention, but also carry the potential for novel, 'alternative' forms of combating social exclusion.

Labour should consider launching an encompassing and innovative social economy programme, but one with a light governmental touch, leaving a great deal to local actors within a framework of democratic decision making. For example, regional, or city-based, social inclusion commissions could be established, with an elected Chair from a widely-drawn membership of relevant local organisations. The Commissions would audit local service needs, propose rules for action, invite and consider applications for funding, liaise with the local authorities and other economic interest groups, and so on. The government thus would play a 'facilitative' role, providing, for example, resources and legislation, but not a direct steer on local priorities and projects.

From regional assemblies to the politics of participation

This last example suggests that region-building cannot stop short of encouraging new political practices at the local level (and, for that matter, at the national level). Labour, with its plans for devolution, is clearly aware of the importance of decentralising power to the regions through the establishment of regional assemblies or Parliaments (in Scotland and Wales), and the restoration of local authority powers so undemocratically stripped away by the Conservatives. But, here too, there is an opportunity for Labour to extend its reforms to embrace the political principles associated with the new European Social Model, namely a democratic and interactive pluralism that draws in both state and non-state institutions.

It would be an error to simply substitute the Tory tradition of placing Whitehall or unelected quangos in the regions by a sort of top-down regional corporatism that distributes power among a small elite of elected and unelected organisations, drawn from the regional government offices, local authorities, development agencies, TECs, business leadership, and perhaps even Mayors wielding extraordinary powers. Governance in institutionally thin regions has always been in the hands of elite coalitions, and the resulting institutional sclerosis has been a source of economic failure, acting as a block on innovation, and on the distribution of resources and opportunity. In an increasingly global economy, while the elites and their charismatic leaders may well help regions to jostle for influence among national and EU decision-makers, or help them to market themselves for international investment, they are ill-equipped to favour a growth path based on unlocking local potential.

This is why it is vital that Labour's proposed regional assemblies or parliaments do not end up as self-serving political institutions, albeit elected ones. They should extend the roll well beyond the professional politician, and draw in - perhaps through specialist committees - experts and representatives from the various professional and civic groups that make up local society. The principle of inclusion, taken seriously, should make special effort to draw in minority and excluded interests. In addition, special attention ought to be paid to how business is conducted, in order to allow full and proper debate, potential for creative decisions, empowerment of the dialogically disadvantaged, and open and transparent interaction with the public and other representative institutions. These same rules of democratisation, perhaps enforced through the regional assemblies, should be encourged within local government and other public sector organisations, in order both to unlock innovation based on voice, and restore public confidence.

But, ultimately, the process of region-building has to spread well beyond the existing and new official political institutions. The prosperous regions of continental Europe are also regions of participatory politics, active citizenship, civic pride, and intense institutionalisation of collective interests - of society brought back into the art of governance. Within them, associational life is active, politics are contested, public authorities and leaders are scrutinised, public space is considered to be shared and commonly owned, and a strong culture of autonomy and self-governance seeps through local society. Labour can do much to help reconstruct local civic society in Britain by encouraging popular projects, the recovery of local public spaces, community development programmes, initiatives to reintegrate the socially excluded, schemes involving public participation, investment in the social infrastucture, civic educational programmes, and so on. These are projects which need public involvement and imagination, but also sustained investment - one reason why Labour's devolution plans ought to include tax-raising powers, so that the local assemblies and authorities can fund the projects.

Back to the macroeconomy

No amount of imaginative region-building will be able to sustain a spiral of endogenous economic growth in the absence of a conducive macroeconomic framework. Inter-regional competition in a Europe in recession, and dominated by restrictive macroeconomic policies, will continue to work in favour of the core regions. Therefore, something has to be done to secure the less favoured regions sufficient time and resources to implement boot-strapping reforms. But even this hope has to be set against the sobering reality that the intrinsic property of the market economy is to produce winners and losers, which makes the elimination of regional inequality virtually impossible.

Such is the history of member state commitment to the agreed terms of European integration - from monetary stability to belief in the market - that the short-term prospect of reversing many of the EU macroeconomic agreements (except now perhaps the schedule for monetary union) is dim. Inflationary, or deficit-inducing, expenditure programmes steered towards the less favoured regions are likely to be blocked. Yet, it is imperative that the European economy, with its alarmingly high levels of unemployment, is given an expansionary kick start. Historically, governments have implemented Keynesian, demand-led recovery programmes by financing public building and infrastructure programmes, as well as relaxing investment and credit restrictions in order to stimulate expenditure, and consequently, industrial expansion. With careful regulation of potential inflationary outcomes, there is no reason why controlled expansion of the economy along these lines is not possible. Without it, there can be little scope for redistributing jobs and economic opportunity to the regions.

In addition, regional financial security, decoupled from the ideological whims of centralising governments, needs to be provided on an European scale, in order to adequately resource policy priorities and meet the income and welfare needs of the local population. Labour, with like-minded governments in Europe, could campaign to raise the level of funding available under EU regional policy. Controversially, it might support as bold a step as a mechanism of fiscal transfers to the regions aligned to local incomes. In this way, tax revenue pooled at the European level can be automatically, and continually, redirected to the regions. Such a regionally equitable fiscal system would ensure that Europe's less favoured regions are compensated for their inability to generate as high a level of local tax revenue as their more prosperous counterparts. But, this is to assume that Labour is willing to explore the merits of financial federalism. Perhaps the moment has arrived to slip out quietly through the back door.

I am grateful to Ray Hudson for his perceptive observations on an earlier draft.

Labour landslide hits Dordogne

'Garçonn - oncore oon gin!'
The Ribérac Conservative Association
is in shock, taking it hard, in the Café
Des Deux Champignons, though mounting
a spirited defence against disaster.

'En Grand Bretagne, le Parti Travailliste...'
On Radio France, they're taking it
theoretically - excited by the Latin root:
trepalium, an instrument of torture,
suggests concern with suffering.

In Ribérac, they know about suffering:
they feel betrayed. You'd have thought
it'd be safe to turn your back...
Maybe the proxy sabotaged your vote.
'Oncore oon gin!'

Labouriste. The 'iste' is taken to imply
a philosophical position. No one remarks
it doesn't have an 'ist' in English.
Labourer: to plough up the land.
Etre en travail: about to give birth.

In the Deux Champignons, upper lips
are stiffening by the glass. Fellow's said
he won't raise taxes ... storm in the proverbial.
'Ploo ça chonge. Que sera sera.'
Gin will be gin will be gin.

Carole Satyamurti

New gender contract?

Jean Gardiner

The 1st May 1997 was an important watershed in the feminisation of politics in Britain. The gender imagery of election night was more striking than many of us were expecting. At count after count we watched Labour women defeating Conservative men. This election also marked a closing of the gender gap in votes for Labour. For the first time ever, Labour's 45 per cent share of the national vote was divided equally between women and men. Although the UK ratio of one female to every four male MPs is still less than in some other countries, there is an expectation that the feminising of the House of Commons and the Cabinet will have an impact on the nature and style of politics. Yet, so little attention was paid to the feminisation of Labour politics that was quietly taking place in the pre-election period that it is still hard to judge what the impact will be.

The election campaign itself certainly did not prepare us for a new feminist politics. A Fawcett report on election coverage during one week of the campaign found that 84 per cent of people appearing on TV election news were men and 93 per cent of professionals and experts called on for comments were men (*The Guardian*, 24 April 1997). There was little evidence of feminist perspectives being explicitly integrated into New Labour's policy commitments, apart from the generalised commitments to health, education, and social justice. Certain aspects of the Labour election campaign were particularly problematic for women, for example the focus on 'welfare-to-work' - the primary expression to date of New Labour's intention to modernise social security and the welfare state. Although Harriet Harman has been appointed as Secretary of State for Social Security, and has also been given responsibility for Women's Issues, there is concern about the extent to which feminism and welfare modernisation within the Labour government are engaging with each other. It is worth considering how Harriet Harman and her colleagues are going to bring these two strands together and how feminists and women's groups outside parliament can assist in this process. A clear commitment to making women's concerns a central part of the development of social security strategy would provide some reassurance to the women's organisations who argued for the establishment of a high profile single full-time post of Minister for Women. Providing women with access to jobs and childcare must be part of a strategy to address women's and children's poverty. But we also need to reconsider the balance between family and social care, and between paid and unpaid work. Welfare-to-work is a less than helpful concept in this context.

Welfare-to-work

As Margaret Thatcher demonstrated, pre-election political slogans are at their most effective when cutting through or side-stepping complex argument. Slogans work best if they make political solutions to social and economic problems seem simple and obvious. 'Welfare-to-work' developed in this pre-election context. But post-election political language needs greater subtlety and sensitivity to the complexities of policy development, acceptance and implementation. Looked at in this light, 'welfare-to work' is not just problematic but offensive to many women, especially those who find themselves labelled as welfare dependent lone parents because the fathers of their children have left them to raise a family singlehanded. The Labour government would be well advised quietly to drop the slogan and to start acknowledging the value of women's unpaid work to the economy and society.

There are at least three problems with the concept of 'welfare-to-work' in this context. The first is that 'welfare' is constructed in purely negative terms. The second is that 'work' is equated with paid work, and there is no recognition of the contribution of unpaid work to social welfare. The third is the failure to link the debate about welfare with the question of how children are raised.

In 'welfare-to-work', welfare is equated with a negative concept of dependency which is perceived to undermine self-reliance and people's incentive to save and to 'work'. It is grounded in the neoclassical economic notion that society comprises autonomous individuals free to trade time and skills for money and each to maximise their individual material welfare. Neoclassical economic man comes into the world fully formed, healthy and able-bodied at 18 or 21 and disappears from that world before he gets ill and dependent or is called upon to take care of his children or parents. The welfare state is blamed for encouraging people not to work, and to spend rather than save for the future. This is a highly gendered and individualistic notion of society, which fails to account for people's responsibility for and desire to care for children, the sick and elderly family members.

The opportunity to rely on others for an adequate quality of life, at those stages of our life when we are dependent, is as much a feature of a good society as the opportunity to be self reliant. We need to recognise that for many, dependency on welfare benefits is the result of commitment to the unpaid work of caring for others who are dependent on them. If we wish to value thrift and hard work positively, as welfare-to-work implies, should we not recognise that necessary unpaid work should also be valued? 'Welfare-to-work' is an example of the problematic way in which, as Jane Lewis has pointed out, the contribution of unpaid caring work to social welfare is ignored.[1] Reducing the benefits bill and providing individuals with greater financial independence and access to jobs and routes out of poverty are only part of the equation. The New Labour government sees itself as a government for the future. This requires strategic thinking about how children can be cared for and educated in a socially inclusive way. Social security discussions have focused on improving incentives to work and save. But do we not also want to see men and women encouraged to be active parents? Signing up to the Social Chapter, with its entitlement to 12 weeks unpaid parental leave, is a welcome first step. But there is much more to be done, as will be discussed below.

Labour should be developing a positive concept of welfare which encompasses a decent quality of life for children and the elderly. In practical terms the focus of welfare spending could be redirected to meeting these ends as spending on unemployment declines. Social welfare should also be based on a partnership between households, the state, the voluntary and private sectors, all of which can be seen to have complementary roles.

Putting unpaid domestic work on the political agenda

For over two hundred years feminists have highlighted the relationship between sexual oppression and inequality and women's responsibility for children and unpaid domestic work. Many reforms have been won, some as a direct result of feminist campaigns, which have enhanced women's rights in respect of fertility, marriage and divorce, and access to financial independence and earnings. In

---

1. J. Lewis, 'Gender and the development of welfare regimes', *Journal of European Social Policy*, vol. 2, no. 3, 1992.

recent years there has been some progress towards men taking a greater share of unpaid domestic work. But women in full-time jobs still spend eight hours a week more than men on housework, cooking and shopping and have less free time, particularly at weekends.[2] And the gap between men's and women's free time widens for those who have dependent children, as women continue to pick up a larger share of the extra unpaid work that comes with having children. By 1993, 22 per cent of households with children were headed by a lone parent and 91 per cent of lone parents were women. Women also do most of the informal caring for elderly people. The gender division of work within households continues to have a major impact on most women's ability to earn, to manage their own lives and to have a political voice.

An important first step in putting unpaid work on the political agenda is to get politicians to stop equating work with paid employment. Such a change of language would not cost any money but would be an important signal to millions of women that the Labour government sees beyond its traditional narrowly defined and exclusive concept of Labour. The concepts of New Labour should include a socially inclusive concept of work.

We also need to have a debate about which aspects of unpaid work can and should be reduced by the provision of socially or commercially provided childcare and other care programmes and which aspects of unpaid work should be supported by flexible labour market arrangements and social security benefits which recognise and support parents and carers. There are a number of alternative models for addressing these issues which have been tested out in Europe, North America, Australia and elsewhere. We can learn from the diversity of this experience and work towards a national consensus on the best policies for Britain.

For example the French system, which initially developed in a political environment in which people were being encouraged to have more children, has allowed women choice about how to balance responsibility for children and employment. Generous redistribution from childless families to those with children is combined with good childcare provision for working parents. The Swedish model, initially developed in an egalitarian political context in which women were being encouraged into the labour market in the 1970s and 80s, combines good parental leave and reduced hours entitlements for parents with good childcare provision.

---

2. Central Statistical Office, *Social Trends* 26, HMSO, London 1996, p216.

With the rise in unemployment in Sweden in the 1990s, particularly amongst women, there has been a move towards more flexibility and choice with the introduction of a 'care subsidy allowance' payable to parents whether in or out of the labour market.[3] Previously subsidies were only payable for childcare centres (where both parents were working or studying for at least 20 hours), for childminders or for parental leave from employment if children were under one. Although in many respects the most generous welfare state model for women in the world, it has been argued that the egalitarian Swedish model of the 1970s and 1980s did not offer the same flexibility of choice as the parental French model.[4] Whilst women in Sweden were offered greater access to political power and lower wage differentials than elsewhere, they also experienced a highly gender segregated occupational structure. Private sector companies appear to have opted to minimise the risk of having people in top jobs taking parental leave by employing men rather than women. This has made women particularly vulnerable to job losses in the public sector.

This election provides an opportunity for Britain's traditional 'male-breadwinner' welfare state regime to be reconstructed. The development of a new type of welfare state requires debate about the different ways in which the state can support people to combine jobs and care responsibilities and about the criteria on which different welfare models should be evaluated. For example, what will be their impact on poverty, social and gender equality, and on economic growth and public finance?

Rethinking the relationship between paid and unpaid work

National and local childcare strategies will need to develop out of partnerships between government, providers of childcare (including households), and businesses whose current and potential employees and customers are parents and children. Some employers are already subsidising their employees' childcare costs, because this has been demonstrated to be cost effective in retaining skilled staff. There are already models at a local level for public-private childcare partnerships and these could be encouraged further.

The Labour government already has some elements of a childcare strategy in

---

3. S. Gustafsson, 'Childcare and types of welfare states', in D. Sainsbury (ed.), *Gendering Welfare States*, Sage, London 1994, p53.
4. J. Lewis (see note 1), p170.

place with its plans for more integrated nursery centres providing care and education and for an expansion of after-school clubs. Childcare and training advice will be offered to lone parents, linked into the individual learning accounts and the welfare-to-work scheme. The proposed expansion of childcare and support for lone parents to gain training and employment are very positive developments. However the plans announced so far have sparked concerns that lone parents, once their children are at school, will be forced to accept job offers which they do not want to take or will be penalised for not doing so. This is obviously not an approach which will help develop a sense of partnership between parents, government and employers. It makes little sense in a context of continuing high unemployment to force unwilling parents into jobs that prevent them having time with their children, and for which high childcare costs are incurred.

Whilst after-school clubs are needed and wanted by many parents, most parents express a preference for family care of young children after school hours.[5] An even bigger problem for many parents, which is yet to be addressed, is that of school holidays. School holidays take up at least 13 out of 52 weeks in the year, and different schools may set different dates, creating additional problems for parents with several children. Moreover, the work involved in being a parent changes as children grow up, and making sure that there is time to listen and communicate is just as important as ensuring physical care. This places major demands on parents, especially if they are bringing up children alone. Whilst better childcare is needed it has to be complemented by allowing parents time for family care.

Whilst economic growth and increased demand are key factors in reducing unemployment, we should also be looking at the important question of job creation and unpaid work in an integrated way. How could the number of skilled jobs be increased by reducing the working hours of people in skilled posts - for example in many professional and managerial occupations where job insecurity and working hours have increased significantly in recent years? How could job sharing in higher level and skilled occupations be encouraged to facilitate both job creation and the opportunity for parents and other carers to combine careers with unpaid caring work?

---

5. Office of Population, Censuses and Surveys, *Day care services for children*, HMSO, London 1994, p105.

It should not be beyond the wit of creative and entrepreneurial employers to make available more jobs that can be carried out between 9 am and 3 pm and which are of sufficient value to provide a reasonable income. Moreover, developments in information technology and telecommunications open up enormous potential for greater flexibility in the timing and location of work. The potential for homes and community centres to be networked with workplaces will increase very rapidly in the coming period. When there are very young children in a household, needing constant supervision, most parents need the opportunity to work away from home and bring as little of their paid work home as possible. On the other hand, for parents with teenagers there is a lot to be said for having the flexibility to work from home for part of the week, so that work can be interrupted when the parent is needed. And where children are at nursery or school, parents could have the flexibility to work from home occasionally, when children are off school through sickness or during school holidays.

If labour market flexibility was redefined in these ways to include scope for parents and carers to negotiate family-friendly hours and work at a distance, there would be greater scope for employers to recognise and value the skills acquired through unpaid work, and the transferability of skills between household and the workplace. Women would begin to feel rewarded rather than penalised for the hard work they put into their active commitment to parenting and the labour market.

One practical idea could be a charter for good employment practice linked into company taxation policy. Firms could be encouraged to offer flexibility of working time to their workforce, to allow for both household care responsibilities and for time off for training and personal development (so that all employees would be able to benefit). Employers could offer greater flexibility for parents and carers at all levels of skill, for example reduced hours, working from home, parental leave and career breaks. Firms which implemented the charter of good practice could have their national insurance contributions or tax reduced, recognising that support for the household care economy reduces the costs of social care. Firms and trade unions would be able to monitor the costs and benefits over time of committing to the charter. As well as society-wide benefits, there could be benefits for the firm, such as improved retention of skilled labour, lower absenteeism and improved health and productivity. By linking time for care with opportunities for training and development, the charter could bring about a shift in the culture of the workplace towards recognising the potential of time away from work as a positive investment for the individual, the firm and the economy. More employers need to recognise that caring for a family can enrich performance at work rather than detract from it, because of the way this experience enhances interpersonal and organisational skills.

There is no doubt that women in Britain, as elsewhere, retain responsibility for the bulk of unpaid work within households and that, in so far as women have achieved greater economic equality with men in the labour market, this has either been secured at the cost of working excessively long hours or has discouraged increasing numbers of women from becoming parents. However it is also the case that, ironically, the absence of a national childcare programme in Britain, and the ad hoc pattern of mostly part-time work for women with young children, has forced married and cohabiting men to take more responsibilty for looking after their children than is the case in most other countries, especially in working-class households.[6] Unemployment in the 1980s and 1990s also gave many men an opportunity to play a more active role as parents and grandparents. These experiences have begun to have an impact on gender identities. More and more men now resent the way pressures of work prevent them from spending time with their families.

———————————

Many women who have been touched by feminism over the last thirty years must have been excited to see women transforming the image of Parliament. New Labour is to be congratulated for bringing about such a significant change and for taking the House of Commons ahead of many other powerful British institutions in terms of its gender balance. A recent feature on powerful women (Natasha Walter, 'Hard labour', *The Guardian* 28, May 1997) asked why there were still so few women in positions of influence, and where were all the missing women, the products of postwar higher education and the 1970s feminist movement. Perhaps it is time for us to reclaim some political space outside Parliament as well. There are many issues a revitalised women's movement linked with women in Parliament might address. Working for strategic alliances and partnerships around childcare, unpaid work, employment, and the welfare state might be a good place to start.

———————————

6.   OPCS (see note 5), p18.

Getting food right

Tim Lang

Labour faces a considerable challenge in food policy. No sector comes with more 'leave it to industry' baggage, yet few can rival it for its capacity to wound governments. Labour was elected with a broad range of commitments, from animal welfare improvement to reform of the Common Agricultural Policy (CAP). Many of them are good, some worthy and some daunting. The CAP reform, for example, will require formidable diplomacy to implement. Until spring 1996, and the dreadful *E coli* deaths in Wishaw, Scotland, there was precious little detail on the party's major commitment to set up a Food Agency, apart from a couple of pages of press release. Thankfully, after years of fruitless outside pressure on shadow agriculture spokespeople to get their act together on food quality, Tony Blair's office did take matters into its own hands by asking Professor Philip James of the Rowett Research Institute to come up with plans for setting up a food agency to monitor food safety.

Phil James delivered his part of the bargain, producing a brilliant model for the Food Agency, which was welcomed by the new Prime Minister in the first week of office and put promptly out for consultation. The process of change was pledged in Labour's first Queen's Speech. This could be the first fundamental reform of the state machine since the Ministry of Agriculture, Fisheries and Food (MAFF) was created after World War Two, and could herald a shift from the Tory era which gradually privatised, quango-ised and generally eroded the food machinery. But there is little point in reforming the machinery if the policies are not also given a shake-up as well. It is this policy dimension that I want to address in this article. Questions abound, from what to do about food poverty (a key factor in inequalities in health) and supermarket power (a challenge to competition policy), to what to do with the rump MAFF left behind after the new Agency is set up.

Food policy is one of those Cinderella subjects which rears its head every half century or so, causes extreme headaches for whomsoever is in government, gets patched up, and then festers till the next eruption. My own belief is that Labour has a golden opportunity to break this cycle of interest and neglect, but only if it develops and implements a new vision. The Labour Party hasn't produced an overall food policy statement since 1985. It is time it did. It also needs to engage with the vibrant food movement which has grown in Britain since the early 1980s. This has captured the public imagination and has gradually hammered out a consensus on an alternative to the last twenty years' policies.

This food movement has a wealth of experience and insights, expressed not just through professional opinion, such as doctors and health promoters, but increasingly through a well run, intelligent alliance of Non Governmental Organisations (NGOs), including the National Food Alliance which focuses upon food and health, the National Heart Forum focusing on heart disease, the Sustainable Agriculture, Food and Environment Alliance concentrating on farming, and the UK Food Group serving the development and internationalist issues.

Well organised though these are, many of their ideas have been formed in the oppositional politics of the Tory era. Everyone now faces the challenge of trying to get change from a government elected with a massive progressive mandate but vague ideas. Labour's food policy could drown in the complexity of the task or merely continue the Tory 'leave it to business' policy. A good starting point might be the insight that earlier generations assumed, but which got lost in the great era of consumption 1960-90 - J K Galbraith's 'culture of contentment' - namely that it is better to assume there is a conflict of interest over food rather than a consensus.

History shows that food policy is almost always a contested space in public policy, a battleground of competing interests and ideologies. Less so in war-time, but even then the rule holds, as we can learn from William Beveridge's magnificent history of World War One's food policy and R J Hammond's of World War Two's. This is not to say that food is beyond agreement - far from it - but it has to be government which makes the decisions and sets the framework for the conflicts to be worked out. The scandals of the last decade or so were often, but not always, due to government's belief in the marketplace and in self-regulation, yet the history of food world-wide shows that these policies just don't work. Corners get cut. Adulteration becomes legal. Food barons exert excess power. Poor people don't eat.

It seems callous to say it, but we owe this chance to get a grip on food policy to BSE. This was truly the scientific straw that broke the food policy camel's back (see Lang and Gabriel 'Mad Consumers?', *Soundings*, vol 1, no 3, June 1996). Extraordinary things have happened since then on which Labour must take a stance. In particular, most thoughtful people now agree that the intensification of the food industry - from farm to shop - has to be questioned. On 18 February this year, the President of the European Union, Mr Jacques Santer, made an impassioned speech to the Parliament on the lessons he has learned. Among other commitments, he stressed the need to rethink the Common Agricultural Policy (CAP) and to turn it into a food policy. He called for a re-think about methods of farming and about the need for governance to be more open and for consumers to be stronger. The food movement has been saying this for years, but was dismissed as unrealistic amidst the trench warfare about the farm budget. For the President of the Commission to be saying this was quite extraordinary. Where does Labour stand on this? Will it continue to back its intensive farmers? Will its policy be the creation of small islands of biodiverse, organic farming in a sea ruled by intensive grain barons? We shall see.

It's this policy big picture which needs to be re-thought. What sort of food economy do we want in five, ten and fifty years' time? Historically, Labour has been good at facing this task. It was the Attlee government which, with Tom Williams' 1947 Agriculture Act, reversed the policy of imperial reliance and tackled the collapse of domestic food production after the repeal of the Corn Laws a century earlier.

Ironically, the 1947 Act ushered in the intensive production about which there is now so much unease. The chance to rethink it should not be lost. A key feature of this process must be to give top priority to public health, the environment and consumer interests. For the last fifty years, production, and latterly retailing, have been the driving forces. The food movement's critique of postwar policies is predicated on arguing that they have given apparently cheap food and unparalleled choice, but at the cost of making food a key factor in public ill-health, adulterating food supply, widening inequalities, systematically disenfranchising low income consumers and degrading the environment in the name of economic efficiency.

Take just one of these - public health. Evidence is strong that the modern diet, with its increased intake of fats, particularly saturated fats, and processed foods with 'empty calories' from sugars, its low intake of fruit and particularly green vegetables, and decreased consumption of fibre, is implicated in the so-called diseases of affluence, a wide range of illness including heart disease, tooth decay, irritable bowel and food-related cancers. Even the last government recognised that unless there is a national doubling of intake of fruit and vegetables, leading food-related diseases will not be tackled. For the poor, that figure should be nearer a fourfold increase. They cannot afford real food at all.

Or take the environment. The environmental impact of intensive agriculture is obvious. For instance, until recently hedgerows were grubbed up, financed by grants to enlarge field sises, unaware that wildlife would be adversely affected. We can now see that the intended drive for efficiency had the unintended impact of damaging biodiversity. Even this April, a South Downs 250 acre wildlife showpiece, previously supported by the taxpayer to the tune of £25,000, was mostly ploughed up, because the new farmer could get a subsidy of £180 per acre more to grow linseed. Labour has to make this impossible, and to reverse the damage of intensification over the last fifty years. This will require firm resolve, as vested interest is high, but public support for making farming more environmentally-sound is rock solid. After all, it pays for it.

Reinvigorating food democracy

Labour's challenge is to break food policy from the shackles of a narrow elite perspective premised on land and labour efficiency, and to modernise and (re)enfranchise the food citizen. The public demand for safe food, for example, goes beyond the narrow conception of consumerism in play for the last twenty, if not forty, years which judges food by price and appearance. Instead, there is a demand for environmentally-sound production, methods people can have confidence in, not the corner cutting exposed in the BSE crisis or the systematic contamination of food from intensive rearing. One in three poultry products bought in shops is contaminated with pathogens, according to a 1996 Consumers' Association survey. When buying chicken, consumers are playing salmonella roulette, not exerting market power.

The demand for what we might call 'food democracy' has to be at the heart of Labour's project. By this I mean the right for all, regardless of income, race etc, to eat adequately and safely. From the mid nineteenth century, improvements in food have featured in the demands of popular movements. In the last century, there was an epic struggle (*c*1820-1875) to control adulteration and for fair traded goods, to win the right for food to be 'of the nature, substance and quality demanded' as the 1875 Food Act eventually phrased it. After winning this right, the struggle for food democracy moved on to welfare - for services such as school meals, for kitchens in homes and for a welfare safety net to enable people to eat adequately. A common theme through these foci was that the state, both locally and nationally, could ameliorate conditions in the public interest. After World War Two, pressure for improvement declined, as the wonders of the new food revolution brought unparalleled choice and range of foods to the populace. Gradually, food democracy was ceded to the marketplace, particularly over the last twenty years. Citizenship was to be through consumerism.

At first, in the era of contentment, the productionist-led food revolution seemed to be delivering, but the food scandals of the last decade have thrown it into doubt. Even the Chief Executive of J Sainsbury is on record this year as linking poor food hygiene with intensive farming. The flaws in food policy go even deeper. Obesity rates are rising, as is fixation on thinness. Gaps between rich and poor consumers are widening. In this rich country of ours, an estimated one tenth to a fifth of the population cannot eat a diet deemed healthy by government advisors due to lack of money. There is unparalleled choice for the rich, but food deserts - no shops - for the poor housing estates. De-regulation and self-regulation have meant that corners have been cut in safety and public health. People are sceptical about the adequacy of food controls, yet they continue to eat and spend their money in supermarkets. You have to eat. Public confidence in food has plummeted to such an extent that even the last Conservative Minister of Agriculture acknowledged that this is a problem. In a 1996 Consumers' Association poll, 66 per cent agreed that 'the influence food producers have on government food safety policy results in the Government taking actions which are not in the interests of consumers'. Hence the Labour pledge for an Agency.

In general, since the 1950s, food culture - the mores, assumption and social conventions surrounding food - has become at one and the same time both more relaxed and more neurotic. At the beginning of the century, people spent around half their income on food. At the end, they spend around a tenth. Yet this 'success' is now fraught with problems and concerns. There never was a common food culture, but pretence is as thin as ever; it is schizophrenic. Food markets are all 'niches' and fragments. Some people are gaining, others are losing. Food is now a source of alienation and is the key factor in Britain's main cause of premature death, coronary heart disease. Industry spends c. £600m a year advertising mainly sweet, fatty foods while the Health Education Authority has a measly £2m to spend promoting the opposite. The NHS picks up a £1bn annual bill for coronary care alone.

Facts like these have been presented to public attention by the food movement, but so far with too little impact on the political process. Since the end of rationing in 1955, politicians have not exactly given great attention to food policy. A handful of New Right Conservative MPs have been the exception, and their main fixation has been the Common Agricultural Policy, icon of their Euro-hatred. The task now is for the food movement and politicians to understand and listen to the urgency of the case for wider reform and reform which doesn't just impose a blanket market framework.

The starting point can be that the struggle for food democracy is once more very much alive. Always, that struggle is a reaction to changes in the nature of production. In the mid nineteenth century it was to mass adulteration and industrialisation of the land. Today it is to the introduction of the quite legal adulterations of mass food, and most recently to the arrival of genetic engineering. Always the food movement is reacting twenty years after the process of R&D began. Labour could win popular approval if it quietly sets the framework for future food production. Labour need not fear adopting what even ten years ago was a marginal radical critique. It may be still radical but is now middle ground. Very New Labour.

Uncertainty permeates the food system

The future shape of the global food economy is fraught with uncertainties - climate change, population, the emergence of China as a net purchaser of food, consumerism itself. There are competing views of what 'progress' means. The technocratic model sees hi-tech fixes, notably through genetic engineering, as being able to cope with any challenges nature or culture throw at the food system. The sustainability model calls for softer, less intense, more local production and distribution systems. A use-abuse approach argues that it doesn't matter how people are fed as long as there is sufficiency, while others argue that if control passes to giant capital a new era of food dependency will have been ushered in. The political and the technological discourses are closely interwoven.

Even within its own terms, the food industry has big problems. How can it continue to value-add when already almost all food consumed is pre-processed?

With some sectors - such as the retail sector - approaching saturation, where are the opportunities for growth? The Foresight Panel, set up by the Department of Trade and Industry under the Tories and which reported in 1995, took a technocratic approach. Calling for public and private sector partnerships, it identified many barriers to progress as potential sources of uncertainty. These ranged from tensions between public and private sectors and difficulties over transfer of science and technology, to concerns about a weak infrastructure and short-termism in investment.

Uncertainties abound, with regard to consumers' attitudes to technology, and from international competition in the era of reduced trade barriers, after the General Agreement on Tariffs and Trade (GATT). Everywhere in the food economy, companies are on a treadmill searching for efficiency gains. Own-label suppliers, for instance, can only improve margins through efficiency gains, while marketing-driven companies can make efficiency gains and develop value through branding. Food businesses are troubled by these uncertainties. Faced with pressure to be more ecological, and to meet consumer demands, as well to cut costs, companies have good reason to be worried about their long-term future. Again, Labour could rise to this task.

Confronting centralisation

The challenge to British food policy is not just a little local difficulty. Everywhere, food policy has moved up the political agenda. In the USA, the Food and Drug Administration is under attack from the Republican right. In Australia and New Zealand, common food standards are key to their long-term plans to become food providers for Asia. The food barons' vulnerability, exposure, sensitivity to consumer and media attention is not surprising. Everywhere, food markets are globalising.

It is a political convention to accept the reality of globalisation; indeed, politicians vie with each other as to their solutions to its challenges for national economies. All agree on the need to compete within modern global markets. In food, this vision is inappropriate. A third course between autarky and unfettered free trade has to be steered. A subtle, new imperialism is underway, whereby distant lands are encouraged to feed the already well-fed, and where 'the market' is a misnomer for commodity traders and rich trading blocs profiteering, cornering trade and in Kevin Watkins' (now of Oxfam) phrase 'fixing the rules'.

Worry though we may at this process, the fact is that food tastes and patterns are being fast exported to cultures where the defence against them is weak. US and EU fast food companies and convenience food companies are scrambling to enter China and India, vast markets with enormous potential sales. Few have thought whether these cultures can afford the coronary by-pass operations that will result in decades' time. Monitoring and anticipating these trends ought to be part of the United Nations' role, particularly the World Health Organisation.

At the institutional level, globalisation is manifest in the power of bodies such as the UN Codex Alimentarius Commission which sets world food standards, used in trade dispute arbitration such as whether hormone residues are acceptable in meat or what pesticide residues one should find in fruit (never zero, of course!). But Codex has been hi-jacked by corporate interest. Supposedly a meeting of governments, a study of a two year cycle of meetings found a third of participants were from companies involved in the sector having standards set for it. Interestingly, at a time when UK politics is dominated by a discussion about different visions for Europe, any romance about 'pulling out' of the EU should quickly be dispelled by looking at the experience of Norway. For all the talk of retaining its independence - and Norway's food policy has had much to commend it since 1975 - Norway is a signatory of the GATT and Codex and has quietly subsumed its food standards to Codex, never in the vanguard of progressive standards.

At all levels - internationally, regionally, nationally, locally - a new baronial food class is emerging. Who without Christian Aid would know about the extraordinary concentration in the commodity trade? One company, Cargill, has 60 per cent of the world cereal market; the top five have 77 per cent. The biggest three companies in world cocoa have 83 per cent of the world market; the biggest three companies in tea have 85 per cent; and so on. This process is accelerating. In 1989, the top 20 agrochemical companies had 94 per cent of world markets, by the mid 1990s, the number with that market share was nearly halved.

The impact of this global reach passes, literally, under our noses every day. Take the simple act of shopping. In Britain, as our supermarket shelves have got longer and more loaded, so the distance food is transported has increased, up by 50 per cent between 1978 and 1993, despite the amount being transported remaining broadly static at 300 million tonnes a year. Over a third of the growth in the entire national road freight in the same period is attributable to food, drink and tobacco - more than for any other major commodity group. Between 1975 and 1989 there was a 40 per cent increase in the average length of shopping journeys, from 3.5 miles in 1975 to 4.9 miles in 1989. The European Commission's Taskforce on the Environment has calculated that total lorry traffic is expected to double between 1989 and 2010.

When we go shopping, we not only use non-renewable energy in our cars and burn hidden energy by buying long-distance food which has trucked up and down motorways, but, from a health point of view, we fail to burn up calories by being able to walk or bike to the shop. Obesity is rising in the UK and there is little hope of achieving the *Health of the Nation* 1992 White Paper's reduction target. So instead of building exercise into our daily lives, we have added stress of thinking that we must go to a gym and take more precious time (and money) from busy schedules to do so. This is a conundrum only saintly individuals can transcend. It is a structural problem. Like everything else, only a reinvigorated food governance has a chance of addressing it.

So what is Labour to do?

The Government in its early months has been preoccupied with three things: a the residue of the BSE crisis, the bill for which keeps mounting; plans for the new Food Agency; and its plans for reform of the Common Agricultural Policy when it has the Presidency from January 1998. These are all fine, but I want to argue that its work would benefit from having five overall priorities before the next election.

The first is reform of Whitehall besides the creation of the Agency. This is on course to exist by 1999, but MAFF needs a radical shake-up, and the Department of Health's food functions have been, frankly, eviscerated by the last government. Co-ordination is poor and the reflex in Whitehall food culture has for too long been productionist. This must end, and it will need firm leadership by politicians and vigilance by the food movement outside to ensure that this culture changes.

The second priority is to develop, publish and monitor the implementation of a new set of food policy goals, incorporating five and twenty year horizons. Some of these goals are perennial, such as ensuring security of supply for an increasingly urban population, but some are new (to MAFF at least), notably the need to expand the use of environmentally-sound production methods and to reduce food's 'ecological footprint'. By ecological footprint is meant the idea that one should not take the efficiency or cost of a product at face value, but that one should calculate the resources it takes to make. For example, it is often said that British farming is very efficient. In reality, it sucks in resources - often non-renewable - from other parts of the world. It uses other people's space. Oil, fertilisers and chemicals are well-known, but less well-known is the use of fishmeal from Latin America and manioc or soya from Asia to feed battery-reared animals. Thus the land space supposedly efficient farming actually uses is far greater than the apparent land use.

Labour needs to audit British food and farming from this new realistic framework. This would integrate environmental and supply goals and help government meet objectives such as those laid down at the UN Conference on Environment and Development (UNCED). Having triggered the worst crisis in EU food and farming ever, with BSE, the UK is under some obligation to meet the goals outlined by EU President Jacques Santer in his 18 February speech. The obvious way forward is for the government, via the Department of Health and MAFF, to produce a White Paper on food, learning from the experience of the 1992 *Health of the Nation* White Paper. For all its limitations, at least one knew what the last government's targets were.

The third, and for me the most pressing, priority is for government to reduce the dietary gap between rich and poor by giving priority to low income consumers. The Low Income Project Team of the last government (on which I sat) provided a long list of new strategies and actions, but then the Government refused to take its own advisory committee's advice. Tessa Jowell, the new Minister of Public Health, could, with other colleagues from MAFF, pick up and run with this agenda. Ideas range from tough directives to planners to halt the rise of superstores - continuing despite John Gummer's much publicised halt to out-of-town development - via revision of the Planning Policy Guidance (PPG) system, to setting up local action teams between local authorities, health trusts, chambers of commerce and citizens groups.

Fourthly, economic policy needs to be more fully integrated into food policy. The last government surrendered any notion of public service or good to the marketplace. In fact, this meant the triumph of what a report from the Institute for Public Policy Research (IPPR) in 1995 called the transition from a market economy to a hypermarket economy. Four giant retail chains dominate what happens throughout the food system. Competition policy, which is already receiving a welcome injection of muscle from Margaret Beckett at the Department of Trade and Industry (e.g. her refusal to allow Bass and Carlsberg to merge), should be stringently applied to food. The IPPR report recommended that competition should not be defined in national but local terms.

It's no good telling a London consumer that if they don't like Tesco or J Sainsbury they can always go to Morrison's or Wm Low when these only operate in the North. (Anyway, Tesco have bought Wm Low's and stockbrokers are salivating about who will buy Morrison's when the family dies off.) If competition policy is supposed to be for consumer benefit, then let it be defined in consumer terms. A 'travel to shop' distance element should be introduced to competition assessment. This might finally get the Office of Fair Trading and the Monopolies and Mergers Commission to get out of their ivory towers.

In addition, Food from Britain, the body charged with exporting more UK food, should have its remit overhauled. The Tory policy was merely to try to export more to compensate for rising imports. The food trade gap still stands at c£6bn a year. Much of this is for food which could be grown here. Spanish asparagus is trucked hundreds of miles to Britain, when marvellous asparagus is and can be grown here. No-one can conceive of being able to grow oranges or mangoes in Britain (more's the pity!), but if Food from Britain really lived up to its name, it would stress food in Britain.

Fifthly and finally, there should be a long-term strategy to re-skill all citizens about food matters. The last government took cooking out of the National Curriculum; instead there is some theoretical health education and exercises in design and technology, like designing a snackbar - this to give design its 'proper' business edge, of course. Instead, there should be a goal of food education to enhance the quality of life, not just to be a utilitarian goal. We need food classes for all school children, integrating food education from growing to cooking and shopping, from hygiene to reducing packaging and litter in the streets. There is space in the national curriculum already under revision to include this food element. Then, with time, we might really say that the new government has helped build a living food citizenship, and helped rather than hindered the long struggle for food democracy.

The man in the Ford Sierra

What the new government's transport policy should be

Kerry Hamilton and Susan Hoyle

I will chair a new Cabinet committee on the environment, on which colleagues from all key departments will sit, so that we can deal with issues in a co-ordinated way. I hope that we can set clear strategic goals for a sustainable development in the medium and long term, including targets for actions and outcomes, and to ensure accountability we propose a powerful new environmental committee of Parliament to scrutinize policies and actions across government ...

I am delighted to announce that Tony Blair and I have agreed that I should now launch a fundamental transport policy review to look at the actions needed to deliver an integrated transport system. It will cover key areas of transport and its relationship with the economy in general and the environmental issues which surround it. We are determined that this review will be conducted in a consultative way, so that those with an interest in transport have the chance to give us their views and wherever possible become involved in the development of policy. My aim is to publish a long-term strategy White Paper next spring which will provide a sustainable framework for decision-making for this parliament and the years beyond.

Thus John Prescott, Deputy Prime Minister and Secretary of State for the Environment, Transport and the Regions, on 5 June, just over a month after Labour took office. His emphasis on co-ordination across departments, joined to an equally new emphasis on transport integration, was welcomed not only by his audience on the day (United Nations Environment and Development, UK), but widely in the press and in the transport world generally. As in other policy areas, this may have been as much relief at a government doing *something* as at the policy content, but he has undoubtedly also raised high expectations of real action against what is increasingly seen as a major threat to our way of life.

These expectations co-exist however with the knowledge that historically Labour governments have been no better than Conservative ones in tackling these basic problems. Most of the Beeching cuts, for example, were allowed to go ahead under a Labour government, and the maintenance of our railways all but disappeared from its agenda.

British transport policy has been a disaster. Ours is a very car-dependent society - the most car-dependent in Europe, and one of most car-dependent in the world (the USA, Australia and Canada are the only major nations to be more dependent). We have somehow contrived a state of affairs where, for a great many families, life without a car is unthinkable, and would certainly be less rich in opportunity and enjoyment. This unthinkability is not because of a lack of imagination: it is because, for most people who now have a car, to give it up would involve profound changes in life-style. If we have chosen where we live, where we work, where our children go to school, all on the basis of having cars to access them, then the short-term alternatives to having and using cars are truly hard to see.

Challenging car-culture is at the heart of the task facing the new Labour government. Car-culture has been so pervasive of our aspirations, and so ingrained in our assumptions, that governments have been able to ignore the real and awful cost of our precious freedom to drive. They have been able to assert that having a bus-service (any bus-service) within ten minutes of your house means that you have a choice between public and private transport; and they have convinced themselves, and many of us, that even to regret people's consequent (and perfectly rational) decision to choose the car is a gross intrusion on personal freedom. They have deluded themselves (at best) that improving public transport is all the solution that is needed, when there is ample evidence that it is not: we will have to be actively discouraged from using our cars if there is to be any significant shift in the environmental and social impact of transport.

How have we arrived at this point? Will whatever stopped previous Labour governments from delivering their sensible transport policies in the past stop this government too?

A short history of British transport

At the end of the war, the new Labour government immediately put into action its plans for a comprehensive programme of nationalisation. Trains, lorries, buses and inland shipping were nationalised in 1948, and put under the control of the new British Transport Commission, which was charged with their integration. Despite a promising start, a combination of the financial stringencies of the post-war period and the fact that it was only three years before Labour was out of office, meant that little was lastingly accomplished.

The Conservatives won the 1951 election with a disingenuous slogan whose appeal still lives: 'Setting the people free'. The collectivist ethic of the previous administration was replaced by an emphasis on individual consumerism, which helped to pave the way for the decade's extraordinary doubling of car ownership, and for the rapid growth of the trunk road and motorway network. Between 1955 and 1965, for example, the number of cars entering London in the morning rush hour rose by 28,000, while the number of buses fell by 1,900.[1]

The rise of the road lobby was rapid both inside and outside Parliament. The 1950s saw the formation of the British Road Federation, made up primarily of the Society of Motor Manufacturers & Traders and the Road Haulage Association. It attracted support across a wide range of interest groups, from the multinational car manufacturers such as Ford to the car unions and aspiring car owners. Car manufacturing began its rise to dominant status, and assumed astonishing importance both as an employer and through the trade union movement. The T&GWU was the largest union not only in the car industry but in Britain as a whole, and its role in the failure of British transport policy is not a glorious one.

The growth of car-ownership and -use continued during the 1960s, aided by the enthusiasm of the Transport Minister, Ernest Marples, for motorways. But some of the foreseeable snags of this policy, notably the rise in road accidents and traffic congestion, soon became apparent. Marples appointed Colin Buchanan with a brief to answer the question: how could traffic flows in the major cities be kept at a congestion-free level in order to ensure the continued

---

1. K Hamilton and S Potter, *Losing Track*, Routledge, London 1985.

advantage of car travel? Buchanan's answer was *Traffic in Towns* (1963), which indicated that there were definite limits on the potential of the private motor car as a form of mass transport: any town with more than 300,000 people simply could not move all its people by car, no matter how many roads were built.

Unfortunately, he also devoted considerable space to explaining how cities could be re-shaped (e.g. half-demolished) in order to cope with the motor car. The report thus continued to be used - until the 1990s - as a justification for the building of more and more roads, and for altering the environment to accommodate the needs of car drivers.

In parallel with the expansion of the road network came the decimation of the rail network. The Railway Modernisation Plan which had been initiated in 1955 came to an abrupt end in 1961 with the appointment of Dr Richard Beeching as Chairman of the British Railways Board. The Beeching report, *The Reshaping of British Railways* (1963), made provision for cutting one third of the rail network and closing 2000 stations.

By this time, the urban bus companies were facing severe financial problems, associated with the increases in car ownership, the resulting traffic congestion and consequent higher operating costs. A vicious circle of higher fares, loss of patronage and decreased revenue was set in motion. For instance, one 12 per cent fares increase in the 1950s on London Transport resulted in the immediate loss of 60 per cent of bus passengers and a permanent loss of 16 per cent.[2]

Nor did matters improve after the election of Labour governments in 1964 and 1966. Barbara Castle's Transport Act (1968) attempted to reverse public transport's downward spiral, but its effectiveness was severely limited by the now formidable road lobby. Nevertheless, the Act represented a recognition by the Labour government that people's travel needs should influence transport policy. There was also an attempt to reintroduce integration and to arrange regular government subsidies to public transport in an organised way. Large transport operating units were set up - notably, the Passenger Transport Executives (PTEs) in what became the metropolitan counties; they were able to benefit from economies of scale and the renewed scope for integrated planning, as well as from the new capital and revenue grants. Further opportunities for integration

2. Hamilton and Potter, see note 1.

were provided by the Conservatives' 1972 Local Government Act. The new councils co-ordinated highway planning as well as public transport provision. Some seized the day: see, for example, the Tyne and Wear Metro or South Yorkshire's low fares policy.

The pathway was however soon closed: the Metropolitan Councils and the GLC were abolished in 1985 and the deregulation of bus services outside London was pushed through in 1986.[3] (One inevitable by-product of this (and of the later rail privatisation) has been the damaging decline of the British public transport manufacturing industry.) Although the PTEs remained, responsibility for transport was now totally fragmented.

The next major initiative in transport policy following this wilful destruction of the British transport-planning infrastructure was the Secretary of State for Transport's 1989 announcement of 'the biggest road-building programme since the Romans'. This committed £23 billion over ten years (the overwhelming majority of his department's budget) to massive expansion of the road network. However, this pathway was also soon closed. The Department of Transport astonished everyone by accepting SACTRA's 1994 report, which had concluded that most new roads do not ease congestion, but actually generate traffic. The biggest road-building programme since the Romans has been virtually abandoned.[4]

Equally astonishing was the completion of the privatisation of a hundred-plus successor companies to British Rail just before the general election.

Since 1947, virtually no new rail lines (apart from the unprecedented Channel Tunnel) have been constructed in this country, while during the same period 40,000 miles of motorway have been built.

Enter the Blair government.

Identifying the obstacles

There are five themes which emerge from this account of British transport policy:

---

3. Deregulation was promised to reverse the decline in bus use; but far from achieving that, it has resulted in a fall in bus use by 25 per cent. Bus use in un-deregulated London rose during the same period.

4. SACTRA is the Standing Advisory Committee on Trunk Road Assessment. The Department of Transport has now reduced its proposed expenditure to £6bn over 15 years.

The illusion of freedom

At least as early as the Conservatives' 1951 election slogan 'Setting the people free', supporters of private transport have appropriated the language of freedom to justify claims for the car. No small part of their success has been the difficulty which supporters of non-car use have in using the same language to stake their claims. But it has always been clear that the car reduced freedom for some, and now it is clear that it reduces freedom for us all, including the people in the car. To quote the late John Roberts:

> If you give people freedom to move, more or less in whatever way they wish,
> - and if you also incorporate in that freedom a scantly punished ability to kill and maim other people, to consume earth resources in whatever way necessary to sustain this freedom, and to mutilate the environment with the roads and track and the effluence from the mechanised vehicles needed to move beyond a certain distance,
> - if you have a small land area and a high population,
> - if you do not intervene in the way land uses are put together or separated, and in densities that people live,
> - if you have implicitly (often explicitly) different rules for the rich and the poor,
> - if your system of government naturally follows a process of transport disintegration,
> - if you sell off the public assets of your public transport system as a act of faith in a religion of market-worship,
> then you have a problem.[5]

And we do.

The corporate bias of the state

The real villain of the piece (and a most easily identified one) is the road lobby. The huge power this grouping enjoyed until very recently was due to the advantage it was able to take of the state's corporate bias during much of the post-war period. Government liked to talk to large powerful organisations, and this applied (until

---

5. *Travel Sickness*, John Roberts *et al*, Lawrence and Wishart, London 1992, p1.

the Thatcher years) to unions as much as to big business and finance, and to Labour as much as to Conservative governments. The close links between government and the road lobby are easily illustrated: Ernest Marples' civil engineering company was a very successful beneficiary of the motorway programme in Macmillan's day; Frank Cousins, general secretary of the T&GWU, was a leading figure in Harold Wilson's government; Stephen Norris went from being a minister for transport in the Major government to heading up the Road Haulage Association.

The recent decline in the importance of the road lobby is not due to any great diminution of corporatism (despite the apparently permanent exclusion of the unions from the highest tables). The decline is the (almost completely unexpected) result of privatisation, and the consequent end of the road-lobby's monolithic interest in roads alone. There is big money now in railways, too - public money, being paid as subsidy to private owners at a far higher rate than when the railway was in public hands. Corporatism lives, and the road lobby is not dead, just weaker.

The decline of collectivist responses

The rhetoric of freedom, hi-jacked by the car- and road-lobby, as we have already noted, has also been used to promote anti-collectivist attitudes and policies, including, and obviously going well beyond, transport issues. The apparent exigencies of the cold war predisposed Labour as well as (although not as much as) Conservative governments to be suspicious of activities which brought large numbers of people together. This is a very unfamiliar perspective on Britain's paranoia in the 1950s, a much-diluted but still powerful parallel to the McCarthy years in the USA, but there is a great deal of uncollected evidence that shows that official attitudes to the car and to public transport, as well as to television versus the cinema, or working-class gatherings (with the exception of sport), were deeply coloured by the fear of unrest and even revolution. In the absence of a study of this phase, it is not possible to trace its development with any precision (for it does seem to have developed rather than declined); but, together with fear of strikes, it surely also lay behind much of Margaret Thatcher's well-documented dislike of mass provision of most kinds, including, notoriously, public transport.

A counterpart of this 'individualisation' of social need and provision has been the rise of the consumer society, dedicated to enshrining 'privacy' as a leading value in our lives. A very transport-focused manifestation of these attitudes was Stephen Norris' famous remark (when he was public transport minister) that it was unreasonable to expect people to sit next to the typical public transport passenger.

The slow rise of environmental awareness

Conspicuous by its almost complete absence from our potted history is concern for the environment as an element in British transport policy. And this is for the excellent reason that until very recently British transport policy was not particularly concerned about the environment. Even now the nettle has not really been grasped. As John Roberts' exegesis (quoted above) makes so relentlessly but implicitly clear, if we are to survive in anything remotely like the style to which we have become accustomed, we are going have to give up the car. The long-awaited technical fixes have still not arrived, and there is no sign that they will come in time; and in any case air-pollution is not the only environmental problem with cars. This is not to join the apocalypse-mongers: apart from anything else, the more time we spend trying to find a car that runs on water (or some other supposedly non-polluting agent), the less time, money and energy we have to find (a) ways of living which demand less movement of people and goods, and (b) a sustainable way of getting ourselves and our materials about the place when we have to.

The political weakness of the transport portfolio

Most people will remember only two Ministers of Transport (and then only if they are old enough): Ernest Marples (for building the M1) and Barbara Castle (for reducing the motorway speed-limit). They will be hard-pressed to name anyone else. And this is because the Department of Transport has traditionally been where politicians on the way up or down make a brief stopover.

The elevation of transport to be part of the super-ministry portfolio of the Deputy Prime Minister is thus quite against the historical grain.[6] It may perhaps be explained in part by John Prescott's known personal interest in the subject; it may also reflect a new, real recognition that transport is important. If so, it is a sea-change of profound significance. The Department's undeniable political weakness in the past has been no small part of the reason for the road-lobby's

---

6. His new department includes the old Department of the Environment, the old Department of Transport and the Regional Government Offices.

success in promoting car- and lorry-friendly legislation and expenditure.

What should the government be planning to do?

Dependence on the car is at the heart of many of our social and environmental problems, and thus challenging car-culture must be at the heart of the task facing the new Labour government.

We can readily agree that the new government has a mandate for a very sensible transport policy, and that John Prescott seems to be the right person in the right job. In the past, the politicians in charge of our transport policy have lacked the vision, despised the details, and completely misunderstood the importance of integrating and co-ordinating transport at policy-level let alone at point-of-use. As we have seen, they have lacked clout in or out of Cabinet; they have also managed to make themselves accountable only to the road-lobby. They have given little sign of recognising how complex transport issues are, and how closely they are interwoven with the factors which dictate the quality of our lives.

So it is only a good sign that John Prescott has already said that he wants to see a reduction in car-use, and that he will be active in securing that reduction.

So what could be achieved? How different could our world be in twenty years' time? For that is the period this kind of perspective requires.

It could be a cleaner, healthier world. At current levels, for example, 20 per cent of CO_2 is transport-related. Out of their cars, people could be more visible, and we could feel, and be, safer. Children could be able to play in the street. The attraction of living in cities could increase. Money could be saved by the disappearance of car-crime, and of the carnage on the roads. Police-time could be directed away from motorways. Some motorways could convert to other uses. Planning might no longer have to struggle to fit cars into our environment (or to fit people around the cars). Roads might no longer divide communities. There could be more local shops, and there could also be more local deliveries. There could be thriving bus- and train-design and -manufacturing industries.

What could stop this happening? It is a dream-list, to be sure; we know we cannot manage a twenty-year transformation without at least some revision, failure and disappointment. Removing the opportunity for people to drive recklessly might (or might not) merely lead to a huge increase in the even more dangerous activity of hang-gliding; car-crime might (or might not) migrate to crimes against people. And the development of information technology, for example, or medicine, or genetic engineering, might lead to utterly unforeseen changes in how we conduct our lives. But without a dream-list, the transport ship of state will be rudderless: it is politician's job to accommodate their constituents' dreams within what is possible.

But what about those obstacles identified above, which have derailed every other attempt to reform our transport system - the illusion of freedom, the corporate bias of the state, the decline of collectivist responses, the slowness of the rise of environmental awareness and the political weakness of the transport portfolio? If we take the last first: we currently have transport in one of the strongest position it has ever been; as long as the government holds to that arrangement, then lack of political clout will not be a problem.

The next obstacle, the slow rise of environmental awareness, appears to be changing. We are far more aware than we were even a few years ago of the danger which recent transport policy represents to our health: for example, 1 in 7 children suffer from asthma, the total number of sufferers has reached 3 million, and the link with transport activity is strong. Childhood obesity is an increasing problem, which moreover is strongly linked to adult heart disease; and the role of car-dependence in reducing children's opportunities for exercise is clearly recognised in numerous studies. We are far more familiar with the arguments about global warming, acid rain and noise intrusion than we were, and we have already made the connection between these and badly founded transport policies.

The issue of the decline of collective responses is less happy. We are still defining 'privacy' and 'freedom' in ways which support individual action and deprecate collective solutions, and the commercial world of manufacturing and advertising remains delighted that we should continue to do so. Reverence for privacy has contributed, for example, to the steep rise in the number of single-person households - which will account for a large part of the 4.4m new households expected in England alone between 1991 and 2016. One by-product of this will be even greater pressure on our transport infrastructure. Changing these attitudes is a job for the whole government, not just the guardians of our new transport policy; we all will need a much livelier sense both of what we can achieve together and of what we will lose if we do *not* act together.

The corporate bias of the state is as strong as ever, but there are two countervailing weights: first, the main expression of corporatism in transport policy, the road lobby, has declined significantly (because many of its members are now at least as interested in the private railway system), and secondly, we have been promised a broadly-based consultative process. 'We are determined,' said John Prescott in the speech quoted at the beginning of this article, 'that this [fundamental] review [of transport policy] will be conducted in a consultative way, so that those with an interest in transport have the chance to give us their views and wherever possible become involved in the development of policy.' We hope that this very welcome promise means that he will make time (whatever his civil servants might have to say about it) to talk to the poor and the powerless, the people who, in transport as in everything else, are by definition under-represented and under-provided for.

For the history of public transport shows up huge gaps in who is heard. Who listens to pensioners' access worries? Why are public transport timetables still built around the needs of the nine-to-five worker, ignoring the needs of the part-time or shift-worker, the unemployed person, children? Why are those same timetables usually unintelligible to most of the people trying to use the services they advertise? Why is so little understood about the recent mass-migration of women into cars?[7] Why do transport planners know so little about ethnic differences in transport needs? Why aren't journeys to schools, hospitals, leisure centres, friends and shops valued as highly by transport-operators and transport-planners as journeys to work?…

…But it is not our role to represent the under-represented, nor to second-guess what they might have to say. Nor, indeed, are we suggesting that it is the government's job to ask everyone what they want and then give it to them. The government's commitment is to involve people in 'the development of policy', and we look forward to some radical rethinking as a result.

The last obstacle to address is the illusion of freedom, an issue which Michael Meacher (now an environment minister) touched on in 1995:

> If you were to ask people if they wanted to own a car, I suspect that almost everyone would say yes. But if you were to phrase the same question differently and ask people if they wanted to live in a society in which everyone who wanted to own a car does so, I think many would not be quite so sure.

---

7. This modal shift has at least as much to do with the failure of public transport to respond to women's complex travel needs as with their rising economic power.

If you were to ask the same question again in a more emotive form - do you want to live in a noisy, dirty, dangerous, socially-polarised, fuel-filled greenhouse? I think many people would have considerably more doubts.[8]

How can this government help us to re-appropriate the vital language of freedom to talk about a transport policy which serves everyone, and not just car-users? This and the need for a re-definition of collectivism, are closely related and are the biggest challenge the government faces. They are not exclusively or even essentially transport matters: they are essential to all aspects of government policy. The government is regarded as having got off to a flying start on many fundamental issues; its popularity is high. There has been no mention of these extremely difficult problems yet, but if the government does not raise them, someone else will. In fact, we just have.

How about, just for starters, thinking about:

Ways to reduce car use

♦ Introducing tax-breaks and promote the infrastructure for car-pooling and car-sharing
♦ restrict access to towns and city centres: reduced parking opportunities, pedestrianised areas, etc
♦ companies to adjust car-mileage allowances so that there is no advantage in driving a larger car
♦ companies to pay generous allowances for the use of bicycles
♦ companies to organise with a view to minimising the need for travel, e.g., teleworking, home working, flexible working and location policy.

---

8. Michael Meacher, 'Integrated transport is Labour's natural territory', *Public Transport Information*, April 1995, p6.

Law and order in the 'New' Britain

Bill Bowring

Robin Blackburn has described Labour's victory as 'Blair's Velvet Revolution'.[1] Indeed, the new government has surprised even the most sceptical with its reforming zeal, at least in the range and rapidity of new measures. Thus, foreign policy is now to be focused on human rights as well as international development on tackling poverty rather than promoting the free market. Constitutional reform includes incorporation of the European Convention of Human Rights, as well as devolution in Scotland and Wales. Attitudes to Europe have been transformed: accession to the EU's Social Chapter has been accompanied by the less widely noticed but no less significant signing of the Council of Europe's Charter of Local Self-Government. Martin Jacques and Stuart Hall, writing before the election, posed the question 'Tony Blair: the greatest Tory since Margaret Thatcher?' Are there now grounds for revising that expectation?

Some analysts, LSE Director Anthony Giddens among them, believe that Tony Blair, with his huge majority, now has the opportunity to 'pioneer a political philosophy that could influence the rest of the world'.[2] Giddens defines this as a 'third phase' (following the Keynesian welfare state and Thatcherism): a 'centre-left project', combining a long-term perspective in economic policy, education and investment, underpinned morally by 'an emphasis on the traditional family, moral education and to some extent a substituting of new obligations for rights.' This analysis is, of course, consistent with Giddens' view that the distinction between left and right politics no longer signifies, that there are radical problems which demand radical solutions for which wide cross-class support can be built. There is also his thesis that globalisation entails a 'risk society' in which a 'positive acceptance of uncertainty', and the ability

---

1. R Blackburn, 'Reflections on Blair's Velvet Revolution', *New Left Review*, 1997.
2. A Giddens, 'Centre left at centre stage', *New Statesman*, May 1997.

to make successful 'investments in life' are as essential to personal as to national prosperity. Even Blackburn refers to the 'radical and hopeful note' struck by a number of cabinet ministers in their early speeches.

But Blackburn also points to the

disquieting strain on New Labour politics that could easily curdle the hopes which have now been aroused, namely its personalism and authoritarianism. New Labour has often seemed to exult in populist appeals for punitive measures - curfews on young people, the harassing of beggars, 'zero tolerance' and the like. This 'tough on crime' approach often entirely eclipses the supposed corollary of tough on the causes of crime.

What better area in which to test these fears than Labour's attitude to crime control and law and order?

Labour has inherited, in addition to its £200 billion financial 'black hole,' a sad context for crime control and law and order policy. As Blackburn notes, during the Thatcher period Britain became one of the most unequal of the advanced capitalist societies. Unemployment may be low by western European standards, but the poorest tenth of the population are actually 13 per cent worse off in 1997 than they were in 1979, while the richest tenth are twice as well off. A recent OECD survey put Britain in 17th place out of 21 member states in the proportion of Gross Domestic Product spent on social security, health and education.

Not only are the poor increasingly excluded from active citizenship; more and more poor people are excluded from society altogether. Michael Howard s 'prison works' strategy, launched in 1992, achieved a new record just as he fell from power. On 29 April 1997 the prison population in the 135 prisons of England and Wales passed the 60,000 figure - 60,012, of whom 2,580 were women. That is an increase of 50 per cent in the last 5 years. From mid-April 1996 to May 1997 the prison population rose by 6000, or 11 per cent. From the start of Howard's policy in 1992, the increase was 40,606 prisoners, or 48 per cent. In a context where the weekly increase is of the order of 250 prisoners, 29 April also witnessed an announcement that the Home Office is seeking sites for 12 new jails.

Young people - many of whom did not vote in the election - are disproportionately represented in the prison population. There are more than

10,500 prisoners aged less than 21. In a recent survey, half of all young men and a third of women aged 14-25 admitted to having committed a crime.

Britain's prison population is the highest *per capita* of the general population in western Europe, but, as in so many other respects, British experience is in some respects only somewhat ahead of a more general trend. At their recent 10th annual conference, at the Council of Europe in Strasbourg, the Directors of Prison Administration of the then twelve EU states noted an 'internationalisation in European penal practice. There was in all countries a general increase in the numbers of people sent to prison, an increase in sentence length, a parallel growth of prison and alternatives to prison, the toughening of alternatives, the proliferation of new penal sanctions, and an erosion of welfare and educational facilities in prison systems. Traditionally liberal states such as the Netherlands and Sweden have moved in similar directions. There are also disturbing statistics which show that much of the rise in prison population has to do with exclusionary policies of immigration control. For example, the numbers of foreign nationals in European prisons in the 1980s rose by 297 per cent in Spain, 118 per cent in Portugal, and 102 per cent in Luxembourg. In Belgium, France, Switzerland and Luxembourg, more than a quarter of the prison population is composed of foreign nationals, many of them in prison for breaches of immigration laws. In France, 85.5 per cent of new offenders are charged with public order offences, of which about half are immigration related.

In Britain, the increased use of prison as punishment and deterrent also reflects increased public concern. A study published in May 1997 (the 1996 International Crime Victimisation Survey) concluded that English and Welsh society is 'one of the most pressurised by crime'; England and Wales are top of an international crime league of 11 countries including the US. The statistics show that residents are more likely to become of victims of crime, be burgled, or have their car stolen, than any other country in the survey. They also face as much risk from more serious crimes, including robberies, assaults and sexual attacks, as people living in the US.

It follows that the new government has more than the legacy of Howard to deal with - and there is without doubt a change of emphasis and a new language in this area, not least in relation to immigration, as noted below. The question is whether New Labour is also capable of a decisive turn away from policies of increasing social exclusion.

The Queen's Speech had nothing to say about prison policy, and only a few words on law and order. But on 12 June 1997 Alun Michael, the Home Office Minister, put some flesh on the bones in his speech to the Local Authority Working Group on Anti-Social Behaviour. He spoke about the proposals in Crime and Disorder Bill, announced in the Queen's Speech. These were proposals to improve the youth justice system and to combat disorder in local communities. 'Disorderly, anti-social behaviour causes alarm and distresses the public, heightens the fear of crime and if unchecked can lead to escalating criminal behaviour', he said.

> The Bill will be the first major step in implementing our strategy of zero tolerance on crime and disorder ... What we will do is place a new joint responsibility on the police services and local authorities to develop statutory partnerships to prevent crime and enhance community safety by means of Community Safety Orders. We recognise how plagued many neighbourhoods are by continual anti-social behaviour by individuals or groups of residents.

He meant, and could have said, that these individuals and groups were the very same young people so well represented in the prisons.

This sounds as if it reflects a substantive and articulated agenda. It reflects what Jack Straw was saying long before the election. For example, in a speech in September 1995 Straw told his audience that '... in an increasingly privatised and private world, street life remains a crucial shared and free experience, critical to the maintenance of functioning communities and society'. Furthermore, in a passage which was widely noted, often with some astonishment, he said: 'Aggressive begging along with graffiti and in some cities "squeegee merchants" all heighten people's fear of crime on the streets... the result is a vicious circle in which people use the streets less, society becomes atomised and community life breaks down.'

Have his views changed? In an interview with Steve Richards of the *New Statesman* on 23 May 1997, Straw remained consistent as to his essential philosophy. However, he did state that the Home Office is not 'just' a department of law and order, but also a department of human rights. For example, he had already shown a more humane approach to immigration, 'a concern for human rights and justice'. Thus, on 5 June 1997, Straw announced the end of the 'primary purpose rule', to 'make the immigration system for marriage partners of British citizens fairer and more effective'.

He did not expect a fall in the overall prison population. 'I think we can stem the rise,' he said, 'but in the short term it will not be possible to get the figure down.' This means, as he frankly admitted, a continued reliance on prisons which are not only privately constructed but privately run. On 20 June 1997 he announced that the government would allow two more private prisons to be built, and ordered the Prison Service to look into the use of private cash to design, build and maintain prisons that would be run by the private sector. In principle, he said, incarceration should be a direct function of the state. 'However, we live in an imperfect world, and if the alternative to overcrowded prisons is to go ahead with this type of contract, we will go ahead with it.' He also wanted the return of the youth justice system which, he believes, obtained 16 years ago, when kids were 'caught and dealt with ... Now they are not.' He has decided to form a Task Force on Youth Justice, drawn from the police, social services, the probation service, the courts, Crown Prosecution Service, the Audit Commission and others, to advise on changing the system.

He has also announced a rapid expansion of the trial of electronic tagging as a means of punishing people in the community. This means of enforcing home curfews would strengthen the community punishments which will be a major part of the Government's law and order policies.

However, his clearest statement of principle has been that liberalism in whatever sense plays no part in his vision. 'I don't adorn my approach to these matters with the adjective "liberal", but I certainly hope to adorn it with the adjective "effective". Some of my critics are trapped in a past that doesn't take account of today's realities.'

This should not, of course, be taken to mean an absence of philosophy. In New Labour terms, Straw is orthodox and consistent. Straw's 1995 remarks were matched by Blair's December 1995 radio interview, in which he responded to the stabbing of a London headteacher by describing a 'new barbarism' on the streets, and arguing for the 'goal of vibrant, operative communities' where people would accept responsibilities and look after each other. The 1995 Policy Document *Safer Communities, Safer Britain: Labour's Proposals for Tough Action on Crime* announced that 'We are now the party of law and order. The breakdown of law and order is intimately bound up with the break-up of strong, cohesive local communities...' New Labour was committed to 'rebuilding communities and reclaiming the streets for ordinary people.'

New Labour did not invent the rhetoric of community. Phil Scraton has traced the way in which a new language of 'community policing' was deployed, in particular by the then Chief Constable of Devon and Cornwall, John Alderson.[3] His objective was to establish 'democratic communal policing' which would respond to the 'common good' of communities and create 'domestic peace and neighbourly trust'. Lord Scarman's 1981 Report following the Brixton riots endorsed 'community policing', especially specialist training for Community Liaison Officers; the return to neighbourhood 'beat' systems; close contact with community agencies; self-help groups; and community consultation.

The cosy rhetoric of community seems inevitably to carry with it its harsher corollary. By the mid 1980s the rhetoric of community policing, Scraton points out, dominated British policing, and community consultation became a statutory obligation under the 1984 Police and Criminal Evidence Act. But, far from heralding a new dawn in police-community relations, it was welcomed as providing a new dynamic of social regulation: behind the rhetoric of prevention, the police could achieve greater regulation and discipline within communities identified and targeted as problems. The police have labelled, targeted and pathologised groups as 'criminal', 'violent', 'militant'; terms such as the 'dangerous classes', the 'underclass', the 'political subversives' and the 'sexual deviants' have become institutionalised.

It has been argued by McLaughlin and others that the central state has created a formidable discourse which employs terms such as 'community' and 'consumer' in a new way.[4] Thus, the concepts of community, representation and participation have become repositioned, successfully heading off demands for democratic control of the police, and contributing to 'the institution of a totalising community-wide policing strategy, involving the local state.

Indeed, New Labour's rhetoric of community is inextricably coupled with the targeting of dangerous, even barbaric, individuals and groups. This is the inevitable consequence and counterpart of the communitarianism which they have espoused, which is based on a distinctive philosophical position.

The source of this philosophy is well known: the 1994 book *The Spirit of*

---

3. P Scraton, 'Community Policing in Britain: Context and Critique', *Statewatch*, November 1995.
4. E McLaughlin, *Community Policing and Accountability*, Avebury 1994, cited in Hughes (note 6).

Community: The Reinvention of American Society by Amitai Etzioni.[5] Etzioni's communitarianism is militant and overtly programmatic. He focuses on three areas of concern. First, the shoring up of morality in civil institutions such as the family, school and voluntary associations; second, engagement with and reversing of the problem of 'too many rights, too few obligations'; and third, the assertion of the importance of the public interest as against special interests in political life. In the preface to his 1995 British edition of The Spirit of Community, Etzioni describes the politicians, like Blair and Straw, who have so enthusiastically taken to his ideas, as 'visionary people who have seen the power of a compelling set of ideas whose idea has come'. These ideas include, of course, the much-hyped 'parenting deficit'.

Etzioni puts forward his own ideas on law and order, and 'public safety', with the aim of enhancing obligation and 'shoring up our moral foundations'. He supports community policing and crime watch schemes. For first offenders only, he recommends a strategy of public humiliation to allow re-integration, since it would 'serve to underscore society's disapproval of the crime committed rather than of the people themselves... Temporarily marking out those convicted in open court, after due process, seems a legitimate community-building device'.

In a large article which appeared in The Guardian on 28 June 1997, Etzioni expands on these ideas, in the British context. He is rather opaque in his qualified support of community policing, which, he says, '...does not quite cut it. While it is helpful to move more police on to the beat, it is also necessary to change the demographic composition of local police forces so they will not differ too much from the communities they are supposed to co-operate with'. Addressing liberal concerns, he adds: 'Stigma is a useful device for addressing criminal behaviour, unfortunately it ruffles the feathers of liberals'. But 'negative sanctions are unavoidable. Stigma is the least costly and the most - yes, the most - humane'. He is careful to stress that his proposals are 'not intended to supplant the conservative's law and order measures or the liberals' job-creation'. Communitarianism is presented, in a curious echo of Giddens, as above or beyond mere right-left politics.

Etzioni's Communitarian Network has achieved considerable success in the US. Its sales-pitch is seductive, especially to a disoriented left, not least because of

---

5. A Etzioni, The Spirit of Community, Fontana 1995.

its careful distancing from the political right. This is how the Network presents itself:

> The easy part is identifying what has gone wrong with America: the pendulum has swung too far toward a preoccupation with individualism. Too many people shirk their communal and civic responsibilities. Special interest groups have gotten out of hand. Moral agreement has crumbled. The difficult part is finding effective ways to restore social and moral consensus without a small group of people imposing a set of behaviors and values on all of us. We need ways to restore the family, without reviving a 1950s mentality; to stop criminals and drunk drivers, without opening the door - even a crack - to a police state; to curb the spread of AIDS, while protecting privacy. In other words, to restore social responsibilities and a commitment to community, without puritanism or authoritarianism. This centrist philosophy is at the core of the communitarian movement.

The Network has carried out its own opinion survey. Its findings, while surely not to be replicated in the UK, are illuminating, in that they throw some light on the reasons for the success both of Bill Clinton and Tony Blair in their recent elections. A random poll of 792 people, conducted by the Survey Research Center at the University of Maryland in October 1996, found that 54 per cent agreed with the communitarian position that individual rights should be balanced with social responsibilities. Only 15 per cent believed that the main focus should be the vigilant protection of individual rights against government intrusion, while 26 per cent said that what was most needed was to live up to social responsibilities.

Asked what they considered to be the major source of America's social problems, 45 per cent indicated that the source was moral, while only 28 per cent saw it as political and 17 per cent as economic. That is precisely the sentiment to which Blair and Straw appeal.

The survey also addressed specific social institutions, such as the family. 58 per cent of those surveyed favoured the two-parent family where each shares responsibilities equally, while only 24 per cent preferred the social conservative concept of having the mother stay at home and the father work, and 17 per cent said they did not prefer any one family structure to another. On the issue of poverty, 48 per cent of those polled felt that the community should be the primary source of assistance to the poor, 22 per cent preferred a libertarian position of allowing the poor to work their way out of poverty, while another

22 per cent would leave the problem in the government's hands. There were similar findings with respect to education. 63 per cent supported the communitarian position that state schools should teach shared values. Only 10 per cent were against such education, while 22 per cent preferred instruction in religious values.

In a recent interview with John Lloyd in the *New Statesman*, Etzioni claimed he is probably right - that the new Clause IV of the Labour Party constitution reflects his influence, in its insistence that the goal of the party is to create 'a community where the rights we enjoy reflect the duties we owe'. However, he is cautious about reform, particularly constitutional reform, in the British context, which he believes to have achieved an approximate balance. He does consider that Britain, and the US, should entrench social and economic rights; 'The gap between rich and poor is too great. It is destructive of community. You can't get equality and you don't want it. But you should make things less unequal'. Then he adds: 'The best way to go for that is through dialogue'.

In other words, Etzioni's politics are entirely consistent not only with Giddens 'third phase', but also with the contention of many theorists of postmodernism that ethical and political problems are to be resolved discursively, through a re-arrangement of language. An example is Etzioni's June 1997 *International Herald Tribune* article, in which he argues that introducing a multiracial category into the US census would 'help soften the racial lines that now divide America by making them more like transitory economic differences rather than harsh, immutable caste lines'. This short passage contains some surprising assumptions as to the causes of both racism and poverty.

Etzioni's approach has been widely criticised - see Hughes important article.[6] Anna Coote, formerly of IPPR, now special adviser to the DSS, has argued that this brand of communitarianism does not tackle the uneven distribution of power around divisions of gender, class, 'race and generation: 'The argument that the roots of underachievement and deviance can be traced to past injuries and impacted layers of exploitation' can be lost in the quest for moral responsibility for 'failure'. Lasch believes that the logic of Etzioni's argument leads to 'the regimentation of opinion, the repression of dissent and the institutionalisation of intolerance, all in the name of morality'.

---

6. G Hughes, 'Communitarianism and law and order', *Critical Social Policy*, 16, 1996.

For Clarke, the use of the word 'community' could be a prescription for bigotry and parochialism, 'given its attempt to resolve the complexity and antagonisms of an increasingly diverse population through the ideological device of a "regressively imagined people" which excludes "aliens," "lone mothers" and the "underclass" from its naturalised ranks'.[7]

From a liberal, or Liberal Democrat, position, the issues are clear. Conrad Russell writes in *New Left Review* of an interview he conducted with Jack Straw in June 1996. He says he was not much worried about 'communitarianism' or 'social authoritarianism until he asked Straw about his curfew proposals. Straw assured him that these proposals could not possibly be authoritarian, since they would not be impositions from above, but would instead be empowerments of the local community. For Russell, the 'notion that nothing a community does to its members can be authoritarian is positively breathtaking.'

However, arguments for a 'progressive communitarianism' have been gaining ground on the left. For example, Michael Walzer has propounded a vision of 'critical associationism' in which citizenship would mediate the other attachments an individual has and cut across them, in an inclusive fashion: 'It would appear to be an elementary requirement of social democracy that there exist a *society* of lively, engaged, and effective men and women - where the honour of "action" belongs to the many and not the few.' This approach is one of several which criticise liberal individualism, whether from a Marxist or more religious - Catholic - standpoint.

Indeed, it is a concern for ethical questions, and the rejection of the social atomism and egoism of liberal capitalism, which provides the core of attraction for Etzioni as well as for New Labour. This also induced the financier and philanthropist George Soros to launch his recent attack on the dangers of unregulated capitalism. It is highly likely that similar sentiments motivated large numbers of those who voted Labour on 1 May 1997.

So what about the critique of New Labour's law and order and crime control policies? One source of such critique is the critical legal studies movement, which, in Nicola Lacey's words, is 'specifically concerned to dig beneath the surface of legal doctrines

---

7. A Coote, 'A Bit Too Much of a Prig and a Prude', *Independent*, 3.7.95; C Lasch, 'The Revolt of the Elites and the Betrayal of Democracy', Norton 1995; J Clarke, 'Public Nightmares and Communitarian Dreams: the Crisis of the Social in Social Welfare', paper, Berlin 1995; M Walzer, 'The Civil Society Argument', in C Mouffe (ed), *Dimensions of Radical Democracy* - all cited in Hughes (note 6).

and practices; to go beyond a project of explication and rationalisation and to interrogate the deeper political, historical and philosophical logics which underpin the power of law'.[8] Referring to the new relationship between the ethical and the political captured within the discourse ethics of Benhabib and Habermas, as well as MacIntyre's analysis of a contemporary world 'which has progressively evacuated the questions of the moral, the good, the virtuous from political life', she recognises the sense of loss and nostalgia expressed in such arguments, but does not neglect the feminist legal scholarship which concludes that there is 'a need for practices which express values and attachments'. In an extension of such feminist positions, Beatrix Campbell has argued that the possibility of 'community' or a 'progressive communitarianism' rests in the hands of women: 'Solidarity and self-help are sustained by networks that are ... open, expansive, egalitarian and incipiently democratic. Their challenge is to the systems that bear upon their daily life. Crime and coercion are sustained by men. Solidarity and self-help are sustained by women. It is as stark as that'.[9]

Lacey's own conclusion is one with which I would agree: '...the idea that there are ethical arguments which bear on law and its reform, and indeed that law could be less unjust and unethical than it is, remains central to progressive legal scholarship'; to which she adds that '...as Marxists saw, the deep reconstruction of the legal has to be premised on the reconstruction of economic, political, social relations: on massive changes in the configuration of power at every level.'

New Labour seems to be committed to a studied indifference to relations of power and oppression in contemporary society. This is manifested, for example, in the location of the source of social crisis in parental irresponsibility, or in the malicious wrong-doing of barbaric individuals or groups. The logic of this position is the social censure and exclusion from society of those who will not take responsibility, or persist in deviant behaviour. It can only lead inexorably to further growth in the prison population, and to still further loss of public confidence in or support for law enforcement agencies and the courts. Few expect, or even consider it desirable, that New Labour should adopt a marxist perspective. Nonetheless, moralism that is not firmly connected to an analysis of the deep structures and causes of exclusion and oppression is likely only to lead to an ever more authoritarian and regressive style of government.

---

8. N Lacey, 'Normative Reconstruction in Socio-Legal Theory', *Social and Legal Studies*, 1996.
9. B Campbell, *Goliath: Britain's Dangerous Places*, Methuen 1993.

The unions and New Labour

Gavin Poynter

During the election campaign the Tories warned that Labour, if elected, would shed its new image and return to its old ways. A Labour government would restore the power of its paymasters, the trade unions, and Britain would be pitched back into the industrial climate of the 1970s when the labour movement regularly exercised its industrial and political muscle. No one listened. The trade unions were not an issue in the 1997 election campaign. Aspirant Labour embraced Branson and business. Trade union leaders offered the occasional soundbite or were silent. If the economy created mere ripples of debate then industrial relations rarely received a mention, except as an aside in discussions about Europe and the minimum wage.

Even in the wake of Labour's landslide victory, little attention has been paid to the future role of the trade unions under a Labour government. In this respect, the landslide of 1997 holds no comparisons to that of 1945. In the aftermath of the second world war, the power of the trade unions was reflected in their elevation to the status of a 'fifth estate'. In the wake of the 1997 election, the unions have assumed a more modest role. In 1945 the political influence exercised by union leaders was derived from the strength of their base on the shopfloor, by 1997 their political weakness is, arguably, a reflection of the marginalisation of trade unionism on today's rather different shopfloor. At the peak of their power, in the late 1960s and early 1970s, unions had a solid base in extractive and manufacturing industries and enjoyed rapid growth in public and private services. This peak coincided with the end of the 'golden age' of the post-war boom and brought with it attempts by successive governments to curb unions, either through legal reform, attempted by the Wilson and Heath governments, or through policies designed to co-opt the trade union leadership into accepting voluntary constraint. Wilson's

In Place of Strife failed in 1969 following strong words from the unions. The Heath government succumbed to the miners' strikes of 1973-4 and the Social Contract was ripped apart by the Winter of Discontent in 1979.

The Conservative governments of the 1980s, aided by the return of mass unemployment, new laws that severely restricted the capacity of unions to organise industrial action, and a protracted period of industrial restructuring, succeeded where previous administrations had failed. The failure of the print workers' and miners' strikes in the mid-1980s marked the end of an era in post-war industrial relations. The defeats were followed by a decade of union decline. The figures provide telling evidence. In 1979 TUC membership stood at 12.2 million members. By 1996 this had fallen to 6.8 million. Over the same period the proportion of employees in unions fell from around 57 per cent to 32 per cent. The fall in union membership density was most marked amongst male manual workers in production industries and mining. By 1995, trade union membership density in manufacturing (32 per cent) and mining (36 per cent) had declined to levels lower than the financial services (37 per cent) and the public sector (health 48 per cent, education 56 per cent and public administration 59 per cent). These figures suggest that the future of trade unionism in Britain will be determined by its capacity for survival and renewal in what some have called the service economy.

The argument presented in this article is that the social and political influence of trade unionism depends primarily upon the strength of its roots in the workplace. Weak roots suggest 'hollow' institutions whilst the discovery of 'new shoots' provides the potential for renewal. Currently, UK unions are in danger of becoming hollow institutions. The election of a Labour government does not provide a solution to this problem. Whilst the government may encourage employers to adopt a more conciliatory approach to unions, it has clearly signalled its intention of maintaining a firm political distance from them. This creates the possibility for unions to develop a critical, political role, independent of their traditional ties to Labour. As a precondition for achieving this, however, unions have to address the weakness of their workplace base.

The relative importance of service industries within the UK economy makes this sector a useful starting point for identifying the weaknesses of contemporary workplace unionism and evaluating its potential for renewal. This article divides into three parts. First, it draws upon some recent case study research to provide insights into the current state of workplace trade unionism.[1] Second, the article outlines various renewal strategies considered by trade union leaderships in their attempts to tackle the problems illustrated by the case study research; and, finally, the prospects for these renewal strategies are explored in the wider political context provided by the electoral victory of new Labour.

The decline of workplace unionism

The picture of contemporary workplace unionism drawn here is based upon 25 case studies of enterprises and organisational units operating in the public sector, privatised utilities and financial services. The case studies covered workplaces employing 100,000 staff of whom approximately fifty per cent were union members. The research involved 175 interviews with key informants - senior managers, union full-time and lay officers and union members. Each case study was based upon interviews and documentation, including management and union publications and collective agreements. The results of the research may be grouped under four main themes: union/management relations; workforce and union; the role of union representatives; and unions and politics.

The weakening of workplace unionism was revealed by the transformation that had taken place in union/management relations in several of the institutions and enterprises covered by the research. There were four main trends. First, management interests and concerns tended to dominate the local consultative and negotiating agendas. Second, there was a movement towards the devolution of collective bargaining to the business unit and local workplace, with local negotiations assuming a less formal and more sporadic character. Third, employers, particularly in the financial services and privatised utilities, adopted human resource management techniques which tended to marginalise 'traditional' patterns of collective bargaining; and, finally, some groups of staff whose employment contracts had been recently changed were no longer covered by collective bargaining arrangements. There was, in short, a piecemeal process of derecognition occurring in several industries. Underpinning all these changes was a management approach that sought to 'individualise' the employment

---

1. The case study research on the public sector and privatised utilities was carried out in conjunction with Peter Fairbrother, Centre for Comparative Labour Studies, University of Warwick and Sian Moore, Labour Research Department.

relation via the introduction of new pay and appraisal schemes and 'employee care' packages.

Whilst the research focused on institutions and enterprises in which trade unions had a history of recognition and organisation, there were significant numbers of workplaces in which union membership had fallen to very low levels. The 'culture of trade unionism', as one full-time official described it, was being lost. Workplaces tended to divide between the few that retained a relatively high union membership density and the majority whose membership levels were in serious decline. In one North London Health Authority, for example, union organisation in a community Health Care Trust was over 70 per cent, whilst in two geographically adjacent Trusts it had declined to less than 15 per cent of the workforce. In an insurance company, union organisation was concentrated in business units with declining staff numbers, whilst areas of employment growth (such as the 'direct line' call centres) were non-unionised.

There was strong evidence that the local union branch no longer provided an effective forum for active membership engagement. Some union branches existed on paper only, whilst others held branch meetings that a handful of lay representatives attended. Local participation by members was confined to informal workplace discussions, occasional ballots or 'crisis' meetings around issues like redundancy. Traditional forms of collective organisation based upon skill and work organisation had been eroded, with the unions finding no alternative ways of reconstructing the foundations of collectivism. Undoubtedly, the fragmentation of the union membership into business units, the effects of contracting out, the casualisation of employment conditions, demands from management for greater 'flexibility' and the rising intensity of work all contributed to the ossification of union organisation at workplace level. These adverse conditions, however, could not fully explain the reasons for union decline. Paradoxically, examples of good organisation existed where the membership was spread widely across a variety of geographically dispersed workplaces and where, for example in one local government branch, the union membership consisted of mainly part-time women employees. Finally, several case studies revealed that members felt the union could do relatively little to change things at work. The dilution of the 'culture of trade unionism' was accompanied by a sense of powerlessness. In turn, this passivity placed severe limitations on individual and collective aspirations. As an insurance worker, whose company was implementing redundancies, explained: 'Our [union members] main concerns are have I got a job and how long will it last for. It is good to know that the union is there but the staff don't believe it has muscle. We don't want to strike and management know it'.

On union representatives, the case studies revealed across all sectors a shrinking activist base even in the relatively well-organised branches. The conduct of union activities fell on the few, though there was strong evidence to suggest that the most successful and innovative local union organisations had women playing leading roles. The activist core of the union could no longer, however, effectively represent memberships that were spread across a variety of workplaces and often several employers or local bargaining units. The fragmentation of collective bargaining in the public services, the growing role of contractors, and the movement of union members from the public to the private sector, tended to stretch local union resources to the limit. In the financial services, workplace representatives were also over-burdened and thinly spread, whilst having to cope with a growing volume of individual casework as well as continuous rounds of complex negotiations over work reorganisation and redundancies.

The general picture of a hard pressed core of union officers and local union activists doing the best they could under immensely difficult circumstances, was leavened by examples of innovative forms of organisation and communication. A senior manager in an insurance company acknowledged that the union had effective control over communications with staff. The union used e-mail links, bulletins and leaflets to inform staff of the latest twists and turns in company approaches to rationalisation and restructuring; and, in the public sector, there were examples of effective local recruitment campaigns and the better organised branches coming to the assistance of the less well-organised. Overall, however, the links between the unions and their members at local level were thin and over-reliant upon the commitment and effort of the few for whom finding new blood to replenish their ranks was a difficult task. In several cases management had reduced time-off facilities for the conduct of union affairs and imposed restrictions on union representatives' activities, limiting them to the immediate group of members with whom they worked. In short, there were clear indications that workplace unionism was in danger of becoming a hollow institution.

Finally, unions, in all the service industries covered by the research, faced many industrial problems that were a direct product of political intervention. This took a variety of forms, including privatisation, compulsory competitive tendering, the introduction of internal markets and the development of new regulatory arrangements. These policies had a significant impact upon management organisation and their approaches to employee relations. As a consequence, workplace unionism confronted political issues almost on a daily basis. Paradoxically, as the Conservative government reduced the union role in wider political affairs, the state used increasingly direct forms of political intervention to assist in the restructuring of management/workforce relations at workplace level.

There is strong evidence that the acute difficulties facing workplace unionism are not confined to those industries covered by the case study research. Surveys, reports and recent TUC conferences and union seminars have indicated that all unions face a shortage of person-power to carry out recruitment and organising activities[2]; that unions are excluded in many important areas of economic activity with density rates being as low as 11 per cent in wholesale and retail trades, 8 per cent in hotels and restaurants and 13 per cent in the business services sector; and that derecognition cases are on the increase.[3] So what have unions been doing to reverse decline and provide the basis for renewal?

Strategies for renewal

The choice facing trade unions is stark. They may adopt policies aimed at managing their own decline or devise strategies directed toward growth and renewal.

The renewal strategies developed over recent years may be grouped under several headings. Unions have embarked upon internal reorganisation; launched new organisation and recruitment initiatives; attempted to exploit the potential of institutional reform, using, in particular, the levers provided by European directives; and, more tentatively, pushed for new 'partnerships' with employers aimed at promoting greater co-operation between the various 'stakeholders' in industry.

---

2. Labour Research Department (LRD), 'Recruitment - Stopping the Rot', *Labour Research*, September 1996.
3. Labour Force Survey, 1995.

Internal reorganisation has been dominated by union mergers and a gradual push downward of resources to the local level. The merger process began in the late 1960s. Adverse conditions over the last decade have accelerated this trend. Unions have tended to consolidate within broad economic sectors, becoming 'general' unions in the process. UNISON, for example, was formed through a merger of NUPE, NALGO and COHSE in 1995, emerging as the largest union in the UK. More recently, the CPSA and IRSF merged to form the Public Services, Tax and Commerce Union (PTC). Mergers have been accompanied by cost-cutting exercises, reducing the number of full-time union officials, and the introduction of internal reforms aimed at professionalising union management. Professionalisation has coincided with attempts to use information technologies to improve services and support for local representatives and union members. These developments prompted debates about the future direction of unions. In the early 1990s, there was a tendency amongst union leaders to embrace a 'service-oriented' approach to their members with officers encouraged to perceive themselves as members of 'sales' teams offering members and potential recruits 'packages' that included insurance and financial and legal services. Enthusiasm for this approach has waned recently as unions have realised that members tend to go to the 'real' capitalist enterprises if they want these services, and surveys found that members preferred their unions to concentrate on defending their interests at work rather having their union membership assume the same status as a Tesco loyalty card.[4] This realisation was accompanied by renewed attempts, partly prompted by the TUC, to improve organisation and recruitment strategies.

Various recruitment initiatives have been introduced by individual unions. These have been informed by experiences of unions abroad, particularly in the USA, Western Europe and Australia. In 1996, the TUC pressed for legislation to secure legal recognition rights, anticipating a possible Labour victory in the 1997 general election. The new Labour government, however, found no place in the Queen's Speech for a bill providing limited recognition rights for employees in workplaces where at least fifty per cent of staff were union members. Such a Bill might have offered some assistance to union recruitment efforts, though implementation would have been a complex business. Within unions there was

---

4. J. Waddington, quoted in 'Recruitment - Stopping the Rot', see note 2.

also concern that a fifty per cent target might have been used as much by employers as an opportunity, where membership was low, to derecognise. Whatever the case, the delay in implementing legislative change leaves recruitment and recognition in the hands of individual unions.

S everal unions have devised plans for shifting their full-time officers away from servicing individual members, through casework, towards dedicating more time to recruitment and organising activities. Between 1995-97 a number of unions, including UNISON, MSF, GMB and the TGWU adopted strategic plans which set recruitment targets and organising initiatives aimed increasing lay representation in individual workplaces. The TUC organised a 'Respect' music festival in the summer of 1996 as part of its initiatives aimed at demonstrating the relevance of trade unionism to a wider audience of women, black and young people. At workplace level, these initiatives have, as yet, achieved mixed results. The main impediments to their success are the lack of resources on the ground capable of sustaining recruitment activity and the many obstacles thrown in the path of union organisers by employers. Employers in the financial services have, for example, tended to make some workplaces no-go areas for unions, particularly workplaces in which large numbers of staff have been brought together in white collar data processing and direct line 'factories'. As one union representative, interviewed during the conduct of the case study research recalled:

> The company's Direct Line customer services division was set up on a greenfield site. New staff, many of them women workers, were taken on. We secured a few members at the site as a result of internal transfers within the company. With their help, we planned a recruitment activity at a local bar that many of the staff use during their lunch hours. We made it obvious that we were from the union when we entered the bar. There were lots of staff in there. As we moved round the bar, trying to talk to people, they moved away from us. It was as if we had the plague. Management had made sure that staff were too fearful to talk to us. We knew that there were problems at work but no-one had the confidence to come forward and join the union. The consequence has been that staff turnover, so we hear, is very high, much higher than in other workplaces within the company. Without the union to help them, staff stick it for a while and when it becomes too much, they leave.

In their attempts to alleviate their domestic difficulties, British unions have turned to Europe to find new 'institutional' ways of arresting decline. As a result of the 1994 Directive, providing for the establishment on a voluntary basis of European Works Councils (EWCs), 200 EWCs were set up across Europe over the following two years. This included the establishment of EWCs by 29 UK-owned multinationals, amongst whom were BT, NatWest Group and ICI. By September 1996 the voluntary directive was replaced by a legal obligation, though the Conservative government did not implement this because of the opt-out clause negotiated at Maastricht. The works councils initiative was followed by further European legislation that required companies to introduce consultation in situations where redundancy or a transferral of business took place.

These European initiatives were given a renewed importance by the readiness of the new Labour government to sign up to the Social Charter. Britain moved into line with its European partners in relation to requiring companies to establish works councils in those enterprises which employ more than 1000 staff in Europe. Whilst many companies see works councils as a means of introducing 'soft' forms of employee consultation, the adoption of the Social Charter provides an opportunity for UK unions to re-establish the negotiating and consultative rights that have been eroded in many major UK companies over recent years. But there are dangers. Where unions cannot claim to represent the majority of the workforce it is likely that employers will establish alternative systems for employee representation, which may severely limit the union role; and, even where union representatives play a significant part, there is no guarantee that the works council will be much more than a talking shop. Despite these hazards, works councils provide a vehicle for unions to develop their own networks of international links and put together more informed pictures of their employer's business strategy. Taking advantage of these institutional innovations, however, is not a substitute for renewal at workplace level. In the absence of the latter, the union representatives who take their places in the boardrooms of major companies will have no more authority than those staff representatives chosen by management.

Along with the new enthusiasm for Europe, unions have begun to adopt the language of 'social partnership' as an ideology that binds together their strategies for renewal. The language of partnership has echoes of the 'business unionism' model adopted in the mid-1980s, initially by the maverick electricians' union and subsequently by several others. In the mid-1990s, however, the concept of partnership has found some receptive ears amongst managers who, in the wake of rationalisation and downsizing, have tempered their 'macho-styles', in an attempt to restore staff morale with the adoption of softer approaches that emphasise employee commitment, empowerment, teamworking and staff development. Partnership implies that there are areas of employee relations where they may be 'common ground' between management and labour - particularly in relation to such matters as training and the introduction of more flexible forms of working. The problems with the concept of partnership, like that of 'stakeholding', are that it disguises the underlying inequalities that structure the relationships between the participants; and, secondly, it creates the impression that common interests exist where often they do not. Michael Moore, in recounting the experience of US labour unions of co-operation and partnership, illustrates this point with comic/tragic irony:

> The leadership of the Communications Workers of America was so stupid that, in 1992, they agreed to let AT&T start a 'Workplace of the Future' programme in which labour and management would 'work more closely together' in teams, instead of in traditionally 'confrontational' mode. The next year AT&T closed forty regional centres and eliminated 4,000 jobs. The union still didn't want to dissolve the team. After six more months of 'co-operation' AT&T cut 15,000 more jobs. The union still didn't want to dissolve the team - and so a year later, AT&T announced it was firing another 40,000 employees! Only then did it dawn on the union leaders that AT&T were up to something.[5]

Institutional and ideological strategies which emphasise partnership between union and employer amount to the acceptance by unions that they can no longer provide an independent form of collective organisation capable of safeguarding and articulating members interests. Such strategies can only assist unions to manage the prolonged process of their own decline. An alternative

---

5. M. Moore, *Downsize This!*, Boxtree, London 1997.

approach involves contesting areas even where there appears to be common ground, and ensuring that 'services' to members strengthen collective involvement rather than reinforcing the atomisation of their experience of work. On training and staff development, for example, unions like UNISON, TGWU and BIFU, have successfully launched programmes of membership education which challenge the narrow competency based schemes often provided by employers and TECs. The programmes, undertaken in partnership with further and higher educational institutions, have developed critical social analysis as well as practical skills and raised the aspirations and self confidence of union members. Such programmes, still in their infancy, provide a real link between the unions and their members. They could even lend substance to Labour's vague commitment to 'lifelong learning'.

Unions and New Labour

Whilst unions have wrestled with the problem of reversing decline in membership levels and establishing ways of reconnecting with their grassroots, New Labour has successfully moved in a different direction. Ignoring its traditional base, the new political class that runs the Labour Party has wooed middle England and won the election against a demoralised and divided Tory party. Now Labour has set about its task of restoring public support in the institutions that run British society. At the same time it is remoulding those institutions with assistance from business and the aid of the rhetoric of the new management techniques. Labour has appointed leading businesspeople to develop more positive approaches to the European Union and financial affairs, and has moved quickly to reassure those in industry sceptical about the impact of a minimum wage. It has signed the Social Charter at the same time as it pledged to spread the doctrine of labour flexibility amongst its European partners. It has adopted an ethical Mission Statement to guide its foreign policy whilst encouraging Ministers with responsibility for spending departments to 'think the unthinkable' in undertaking reforms in areas like health, education and social security. In brief, it has borrowed the fashionable language of the business world and the ethical values of the Body Shop to dress up an essentially authoritarian agenda, particularly in the areas of social policy and employment.

The cocktail of mission statements and business ethics espoused by New

Labour may reflect the mood that exists in many British boardrooms. The confidence expressed by the entrepreneurial culture of the Thatcher years has been undermined by a lengthy period of recession and restructuring and a bad press in which the 'fatcats' were mercilessly attacked. In response, ethical capitalism has gained ground. This ethos, however, offers little comfort to ordinary trade union members, some of whom have already experienced its effects. The Co-operative Bank, for example, resurrected itself following a significant decline in profitability in the wake of the recession that hit financial services in the late 1980s and early 1990s. In 1991 the bank re-discovered its roots by applying ethical values to its investment strategies. Its ethics stood in stark contrast to those prevailing in the financial world. The marketing ploy appealed to the middle classes. The bank's customer base was restored and replenished. Its business services expanded in niche markets in the voluntary sector and amongst small businesses. Its ethical values were passed to its own workforce. Staff were encouraged to attend 'our heritage' seminars. Since the re-discovery of its heritage, the bank has also shed around 1000 jobs.

The new moral climate created in the wake of Labour's election victory may serve to reduce the overt hostility to trade unionism that has prevailed for several years. It may also provide opportunities for trade unions to re-enter government offices and company boardrooms. Such an 'institutional fix', though, does not provide a sound foundation for renewal. In several industries and many workplaces trade unionism is absent or in serious decline. In those workplaces where union organisation exists it is under considerable pressure and is often reliant on a dedicated few. For the unions, returning to their old ways is not an option. The world of work has changed dramatically over the past two decades. Despite media attempts to suggest otherwise, strikes in the 1990s do not have the same frequency or social impact as those which occurred in the 1970s. Their narrow terms, often designed from the union perspective to 'limit the damage', inevitably reduce their social and political significance and tend, paradoxically, to be illustrative of weakness rather than the potential for renewal. Whilst union activists may argue strongly against the punitive Tory legislation that places severe limits on the most elementary right of trade unionists to take solidarity action in support of others in dispute, there is, regrettably, no evidence of support for the restoration of this basic democratic right within the wider society. In brief, it is a mistake to regard the occasional strikes that arise in contemporary Britain as a measure of the potential for renewal. To do so amounts to a romantic desire to restore or reconstruct the past.

The re-establishment of the industrial/political relevance of collectivism, like that of class, is a longer term project and takes place in what Geoff Mulgan and others have called an 'anti-political' age. For Mulgan, the restoration of trade unions as effective social institutions rests upon their capacity to help re-shape the labour market and assist those who may be casualties of the transition to a post-industrial society.[6] The evolution of trade unions into providers of unemployment insurance and into employee mutuals that sell on labour to enterprises, as well as Mulgan's case for the development of the shared ownership of businesses between labour and capital, contain echoes of the writings of the nineteenth-century utopian socialists, particularly Owen and Proudhon. Mulgan's argument for the reconnection of ownership and responsibility also contains many of the methodological errors of his nineteenth-century predecessors and is no more practical today than it was over a century ago. The weaknesses are, at least, fourfold. First, unions no longer have the roots in crafts and occupations that would enable them to effectively influence or control the supply of labour into specific industries and labour markets. (Ironically, the last vestiges of such controls were destroyed in the 1970s and 80s in areas like shipbuilding, the docks and printing.) Second, their emergence as providers of welfare benefits would require resources and finance that they have not got. Third, and most importantly, new forms of partnership, and joint or shared ownership, cannot buck the demands of the capitalist market, as the recent failure of some mining communities' attempts to take over their own pits has proved. Changing the form of ownership of capital (between entrepreneurs, institutions, the state and even labour) does little to challenge, and often assists in, the maintenance of its domination as an 'organic system'.[7] Finally, the roots of union strength lie in the workplace and in its capacity to challenge the decisions that arise from this system of domination. Mulgan tends to ignore the systemic roots of the differences between labour and capital and

---

6. G. Mulgan, *Connexity*, Chatto and Windus, London 1997; G. Mulgan and T. Bentley, *Employee Mutuals: the 21st Century Trade Union*, Demos, London 1996.
7. I. Meszaros, *Beyond Capital*, Merlin, London 1995.

focus on an idealised notion of co-operation that has little resonance in a real world driven by downsizing and work intensification.

The future of labour collectivism depends upon its ability to acknowledge the basic antagonism inherent in the relations between employers and workers to reject the rhetoric of social partnership and develop an independent political voice within society. The prerequisite for this is renewal from below, a slow process through which organised labour reasserts itself as an agency of democratic involvement and social change, that challenges the prevailing culture of 'there is no alternative' shared by the main political parties. In short, effective renewal rests upon re-kindling the individual and collective aspirations of labour and lending these new organisational forms. To achieve this unions need to reconnect with their members at the workplace level; to challenge the trends toward the atomisation of the experience of work which the new management approaches emphasise; and to develop their own agendas for delivering 'services', like education and training, which require the member to participate as part of a collective group rather than consume as a passive individual. The renewal of collectivism requires patience, and a preparedness to embrace new ways of organising those who are now accustomed to a work culture that encourages the politics of self-limitation.

What health tells us about society

Richard Wilkinson

The social determinants of health

Research on health inequalities is changing our understanding of how people are affected by the social structures in which they live. Differences in death rates provide 'hard' data on the impact of socioeconomic inequalities on people's lives.

Evidence of three-fold differences in death rates between upper and lower social classes, or between richer and poorer neighbourhoods, reminded us of how sensitive health continues to be to differences in material circumstances - even in supposedly affluent developed countries. As research has continued over the last fifteen or twenty years, it has become clear that this mortality gradient results less from the *direct* effect of differences in people's material circumstances than it does from the psychosocial effects of those differences. Although factors such as damp housing and inner city air pollution do have direct effects on health, much more important are the health effects of people's subjective experience of their position in society - whether it makes them feel successful, optimistic, confident, or failures, socially excluded, depressed, economically insecure and desperate.

The health gradient does not distinguish just between the poor and the rest of society: health standards and life expectancy improve all the way up the social ladder. So for instance even in the Whitehall Study of 17,000 civil servants working in London offices, the most junior staff were found to have death rates three times as high as the most senior staff working in the same offices, with the ranks in between having intermediate death rates (see figure

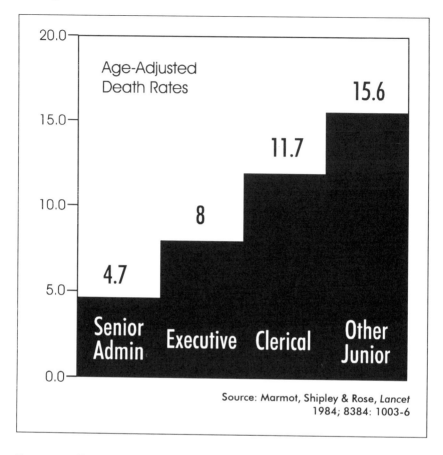

Age-Adjusted
Death Rates

15.6

11.7

8

4.7

Senior Admin   Executive   Clerical   Other Junior

Source: Marmot, Shipley & Rose, *Lancet*
1984; 8384: 1003-6

*Figure 1: Differences in death rates between
senior and junior Whitehall Civil Servants*

1).[1] Nor is this a matter of just one or two causes of death: with the exception of breast and skin cancer, the vast majority of causes of death are more common lower down the social scale.

After the publication of the Black Report on health inequalities in 1980,[2] the first research task was to check whether these health differences were

1. M.G. Marmot, M.J. Shipley, G. Rose, 'Inequalities in death - specific explanations of a general pattern', *Lancet* 1984.
2. *Inequalities in Health: the Black Report and the Health Divide,* Penguin Books, Harmondsworth 1992.

produced by a tendency for social mobility to act as a sorting process moving the healthy upwards and the unhealthy down. It turned out that although there is a tendency for this to happen, it makes only a small contribution to health inequalities.[3] Indeed, the overall effect of social mobility seems to be to reduce the differences which would arise if everyone was exposed to the same advantaged or disadvantaged conditions throughout their lives.

The next research task was to look at the contribution of behavioural factors like smoking, unhealthy food choices or lack of exercise. Again, while these factors are influential, they leave most of the health inequalities - even in diseases like heart disease - unexplained. This is partly because there are only very minor differences in fat consumption between social classes, and partly because behavioural factors are less important than people imagine. Even if you minimise your risks by getting all the behavioural factors right, your most likely cause of death is still heart disease.

Although there are very strong relationships between almost any measure of health and almost any measure of social and economic circumstances, attempts to account for the bulk of this relationship in terms of the toxic effects of exposure to hazardous conditions have met with less success than might have been expected. It is for instance difficult to see how poor housing could increase the incidence of cardiovascular diseases or cancers. Similarly, class differences in fat consumption are much too small to explain any of the huge differences in heart disease. However, psychosocial factors, like having control over one's work and domestic circumstances, job security, a regular income, social support, the absence of 'long term difficulties' and threatening 'life events', the quality of parenting and lack of family conflict early in life, all appear unexpectedly successful in explaining differences in physical disease. As the epidemiological evidence has pointed increasingly towards psychosocial factors such as these, so progress has also been made in tracking the biological pathways through which chronic stress - or worry - can affect the immune and endocrine systems and increase the risks of a wide range of diseases.[4]

---

3. D. Blane, G. Davey Smith, M. Bartley, 'Social selection: what does it contribute to social class differences in health?', *Sociology of Health and Illness*, 1993.
4. W.R. Lovallo, *Stress and health: biological and psychological interactions*, Sage, London 1997.

Social position

This picture - of health linked to material circumstances primarily through psychosocial rather than direct material pathways - is confirmed by recent evidence which shows that the relationship between income and health is less a reflection of the impact of *absolute* income levels on health as of the effects of *relative* income. Living standards for the vast majority of people in the developed world have long surpassed the levels at which absolute material standards are the main limitation on health: what matters now is where your income places you in the social hierarchy. Interestingly, the health impact of social status is also powerfully demonstrated by studies of non-human primates. The physiological effects of position in the social hierarchy have been studied among baboons and macaques. They seem to hinge on the physiological repercussions of chronic stress experienced by subordinate animals, and look strikingly similar to the effects found among human beings in low social status positions. Amongst the monkeys and baboons it is possible to manipulate social status experimentally, and so to confirm that causality does indeed run, as the human studies suggested, from social status to the physiological differences rather than the other way round.

Income inequality

Arising from the importance of relative income and the effects of low social status is a marked tendency for more egalitarian societies - with smaller income differences between rich and poor - to be healthier. In the developed world, it is not the richest societies like the United States which are healthiest, but the ones with smaller inequalities in income - like Japan and Sweden. This relationship has now been found by a number of different research workers, using various sets of data looking at international differences, sometimes at a point in time and sometimes at changes over time (see figure 2). The same relationship has recently also been found among the 50 American states: again it is not the richest, but the most egalitarian, states which have the lowest death rates (see figure 3). The most important part of the explanation for this is almost certainly that greater equality reduces the burden of relative deprivation on health. In effect, societies are healthier where the hierarchy is less hierarchical.

The relationship between greater equality and better health is

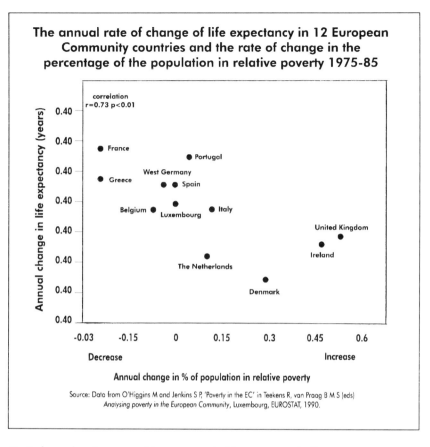

The annual rate of change of life expectancy in 12 European Community countries and the rate of change in the percentage of the population in relative poverty 1975-85

Source: Data from O'Higgins M and Jenkins S P, 'Poverty in the EC' in Teekens R, van Praag B M S (eds) *Analysing poverty in the European Community*, Luxembourg, EUROSTAT, 1990.

Fig 2 shows that the range of improvement in life expectancy in European countries was related to changes in the extent of relative poverty. The horizontal axis shows whether the proportion of the population living on less than half the average income in each country was increasing or decreasing 1975-85. The vertical axis shows how fast average life expectancy increased in each country over the same period. Both are expressed as an average annual amount of change.

surprisingly strong. If, as the statistics suggest, it accounts for anywhere near half the differences in life expectancy between developed countries, the amount of inequality would be the most powerful influence on population health yet identified.

While there can be little doubt that the main health benefits of greater equality accrue - as you would expect - to the least well-off, there may also be some 'knock-on' effects of living in a more egalitarian society which benefit

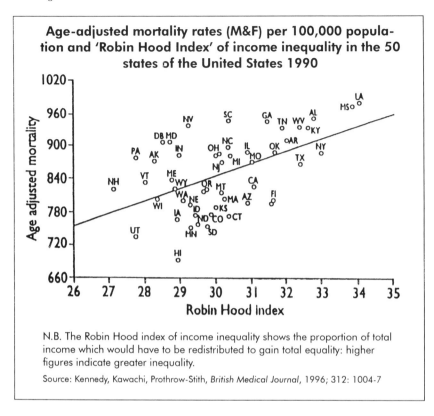

Age-adjusted mortality rates (M&F) per 100,000 population and 'Robin Hood Index' of income inequality in the 50 states of the United States 1990

N.B. The Robin Hood index of income inequality shows the proportion of total income which would have to be redistributed to gain total equality: higher figures indicate greater inequality.

Source: Kennedy, Kawachi, Prothrow-Stith, *British Medical Journal*, 1996; 312: 1004-7

the rich. Although the major categories of cause of death - including cancers, infections, cardiovascular and respiratory diseases - all tend to be more common in more unequal societies, the causes which respond most dramatically (in terms of percentage changes) to the scale of income inequality are accidents, alcohol related causes, violence and infections. These rather social causes suggest that there are differences in the nature of the social fabric and in risk behaviour between more and less egalitarian societies. Even though the least well-off will suffer most from the higher rates of homicide, accidents and infections, the rich are unlikely to be fully insulated from them or the social processes behind them.

Social cohesion

It seems then that death rates reflect the powerful effects of inequality on the psychosocial welfare of populations. But if income differences have a sufficiently powerful effect on the social fabric to affect death rates, they must surely also influence other social problems. It is implausible that major differences in the psychosocial tenor of society find expression in mortality alone. Indeed, the much higher death rates from alcohol related causes, accidents and violence in less egalitarian societies already point the way to other effects. Research has shown that homicide rates are related to income inequality, both internationally and in the USA, where they explain an important proportion of the nine-fold differences in homicide rates in different states.[5] Violent crime is similarly related but, at least in some statistical series, property crime appears less closely related. In Britain, overall crime rates are so closely related to measures of deprivation that it is hard to distinguish between maps of crime and maps of deprivation. Japan is interesting here. After income differences had narrowed during most of the post-war period, by the end of the 1980s Japan had the narrowest income differences and highest life expectancy in the developed world. It had also enjoyed a long term decline in most categories of crime - particularly those associated with deprived areas and lower socioeconomic status. Indeed, only categories of 'white collar' crime had not declined.

If home background has an important effect on children's educational performance, you might expect that educational standards would also be affected by income inequality. In Britain between 1979 and the early 1990s, the proportion of children who came from homes in which people struggle to live on less than half the average income grew from about ten per cent to over 30 per cent. Much the most rapid part of this growth took place after 1985. It is exactly during that period that reading standards in primary schools declined.[6] Three pieces of research all confirmed the decline; they said it had nothing to do with the use of the reading methods which various government ministers had sought to blame, but said that the 'watershed' year was 1985 and that the deterioration was most apparent in the inner cities and in schools with poor catchment areas. In the same period there was also

5. G. A. Kaplan, E. Pamuk, L.W. Lynch, R.D. Cohen, J.L. Balfour, 'Income inequality and mortality in the United States: analysis of mortality and potential pathways', *British Medical Journal* 1996.
6. R.G. Wilkinson, *Unfair Shares: the effects of widening income differentials on the welfare of the young,* Barnardos, London 1994.

a marked decline in the rate of improvement in death rates among infants, children, and adults under 45. Again, the poor performance was clearly concentrated in the most deprived areas.

Educational standards have always been closely related to socioeconomic circumstances, and, if almost a third of children come from homes below the poverty line, teaching and learning obviously become more difficult. In deprived areas three-quarters of the children in each classroom may live in poverty. Brought up by parents coping with the increased stress of caring for children with inadequate and insecure resources, levels of tolerance and patience will be lower and children will suffer more emotional and behavioural problems as a result.[7] Because of the close links between health and emotional welfare, domestic conflict in childhood not only leads to poorer school performance and to an increased willingness to resort to violence, but also to worse health later in life.

A quite different short term indicator of the effects of widening income differences on psychosocial welfare comes from statistics of smoking. As the poor got poorer, it seems that - despite the expense - they smoked more. The continuing long-term decline in smoking among most of the population was reversed among poorer men and women.[8] Just when their relative poverty was increasing most rapidly, the poor devoted a larger proportion of their income to smoking. As has been pointed out, it is hardest to give up smoking when you feel hopeless and least in control of your life.

Several pieces of evidence have come together recently to suggest that part of the reason why more egalitarian societies are healthier is that they tend to be more socially cohesive. I discussed several examples of unusually healthy and egalitarian societies - like Britain during the two World Wars, Japan, and an Italian-American town called Roseto in Pennsylvania - in a chapter of my book *Unhealthy Societies*. The examples suggested that what may be important is a sense of camaraderie, or something approaching a community of values capable of ensuring that the public space is a social space and that social life does not stop outside the front door. The impression that something like social cohesion is involved is strengthened by data - again -

---

7. O. James, *Juvenile violence in a winner-looser culture*, Free Association Books, 1995.
8. A. Marsh, S. McKay, *Poor Smokers*, Policy Studies Institute, 1994.

from the United States. It shows that the relationship between greater income equality and lower mortality rates is mediated - at least in statistical terms - by the extent to which people feel they can trust each other.

The declining importance of economic growth

What these relationships seem to be telling us is that the nature of the social environment is crucially important to human welfare. Since the so-called 'epidemiological transition', when infectious diseases gave way to the degenerative diseases as the main causes of death, the grip which material living standards used to have on mortality has loosened. The decline of the great infections of the past marks a crucial stage in economic development, when the vast majority of the population attained access to a threshold level of material standards. Infections remain the most common causes of death in poorer countries primarily because that same threshold has not yet been reached by a large proportion of their populations. Indicative of the attainment of an economic threshold in the developed world is that, in the later stages of the decline in infections, a number of the so-called 'diseases of affluence' reversed their social distributions to become more common among the poor in affluent societies. Amongst others, coronary heart diseases, stroke, lung cancer, duodenal ulcers and obesity all reversed their social distributions from being most common among the rich to being most common among the poor in affluent societies. Throughout history the rich had been fat and the poor thin, but with rising living standards the poor could now afford to be fat. Obesity therefore lost its association with social status, ideas of physical attractiveness changed, and the slimming industry was born.

The decline of the infections, together with the way the 'diseases of affluence' became the diseases of the poor in affluent societies, shows that the epidemiological transition marks the attainment of minimum material living standards for the bulk of the population. This explains the subsequent weakness of the link between rising life expectancy and economic growth. Although life expectancy continues to rise, how fast it does so now bears very little relationship to long term economic growth rates. Real living standards can grow twice as fast in one developed country as in another for as long as twenty years without necessarily bringing bigger improvements in life expectancy as a result. Having attained a threshold standard of living consistent with good health, economic growth now does much less for us than it once did. Although there is still homelessness and absolute material need, not only is the proportion of the population affected too small to influence population mortality rates, but these problems have re-emerged despite economic growth partly as a result of widening income differences.

A much more important source of the continuing improvements in life expectancy than economic growth are the social and cultural changes which, though partly enabled by the dramatic reduction of material need, sweep across the developed world largely unaffected by different growth rates. The central features of this progress are likely to involve the civilising processes of a general psychosocial liberalisation. Its most easily identifiable outward features - such as the abolition of corporal punishment of school children - are reflections of deeper processes. The same is true of the abolition of capital punishment, the legalisation of homosexuality, the abolition of conscription, the greater informality of social life at all levels, and the growing recognition of the importance of our psychological and emotional development. Indeed, it seems likely that these factors move forward more rapidly in more egalitarian societies. Here the contrast between countries like the United States and Sweden with respect to issues like capital punishment is telling.

Going through the emerging picture of the social determinants of health, you can't help thinking that even more important than what society tells us about health, is what health tells us about society and the quality of life. (But note that although it is easy to be dismissive of a few years extra life expectancy in societies which already think of themselves as overburdened by the proportion of old people, most of the increase in life expectancy has come from reducing deaths at younger ages.)

The social environment

The picture emerging from research on health inequalities might have looked much the same if we had been looking at a range of other social problems, such as violent crime, the educational under-performance of school children, or drug taking. They - and social cohesion itself - are all powerfully affected by the scale of relative deprivation. We are dealing with the socially corrosive effects of inequality on the real subjective quality of life. What the health data tells us is that improvements in the social environment are now more important than improvements in the material environment.[9] Our highly developed sensitivity to the social environment is almost certainly attributable to the fact that the quality of social relations has always been a crucial determinant of human welfare. Think about it for a moment in evolutionary terms: while other species may compete with us for the same food resources, other human beings are potentially our most awesome competitors, competing not only for the same food, but for all other resources - housing, sexual partners, jobs, even the shirt off your back. But equally, our fellow human beings have the potential to be the greatest source of comfort, love, solace, help and fellowship, and our cultural learning is entirely dependent on close contact with each other. The nature of social relations must always have been crucial to human welfare. Indeed, this is likely to be why the hunting and gathering societies which dominated human pre-history were 'assertively egalitarian' and usually eschewed forms of exchange which were overtly self-interested. The reliance on gift exchange and food sharing almost certainly shows the importance of investment in social relations. After all, 'gifts make friends and friends make gifts'. Keeping on friendly terms with other people and avoiding envy and conflict were basic to survival and to the quality of life.

Social development and the market

Faced with the contrast between the 'primitive communism' of hunter-gatherer societies and the anti-social characteristics of the market, we are left contemplating the collapse of socialist thought. At its centre seems to be the lack of any idea of a coherent alternative to the market. The opposition between socialist values and the market has been so central that we have often seen the need to work out a coherent alternative to the market as the precondition for any socialist or humanitarian society. The central problem is the way the exploitative and overtly self-interested rationale of the market conflicts with the mutuality which is fundamental to social relations.

After the collapse of Eastern Europe, if not before, the impossibility of inventing an alternative to the market has politically immobilised many who recognise the need for a more social society. But even market societies can

---

9. The material problems of those on low incomes have increased as a result of widening income differences rather than from a lack of economic growth.

develop in very different ways. It is only too easy to imagine a future in a divided society, in which the rich live in protected enclaves, defended against the violence of the excluded poor by all the paraphernalia of security systems, while the poor themselves are left to hopelessness and the fight for whatever meagre resources are left to them. Fortunately, it is also easy to imagine a more egalitarian and cohesive future in an society which has invested in the education and welfare of the whole population, and, by enabling new forms of social expression, sows the seeds of a more social future. There are already examples of societies which have developed some way in each of these directions. The more egalitarian societies such as Japan or Sweden contrast sharply with the much more violent inegalitarian countries like the United States or the even more divided but poorer societies such as South Africa, Brazil, Columbia and now perhaps even Russia. There can be no doubt that the immediate political task is to ensure that we take the more social path.

In a number of respects we stand at the watershed between these two courses. With hindsight, perhaps the choice of a new government will appear to be the time when the decision to take the more social route was taken. But the political changes in Britain were bound up with the wider demise of the approach to political and economic life associated with monetarism. As an economic theory, it was associated with a pessimistic theory of human motivation and of society. Providing the ideological underpinnings of the political right, it began to look like a played out force before the end of the 1980s. The size of the Labour victory simply reflected how far it had got beyond its sell-by date. The moral and social bankruptcy of the whole ideology had become plain for all to see in the government's disregard for increasing relative poverty and in the frequent signs of corruption in public office.

Particularly timely in terms of the possibility for developing a more social economy is a change in thinking on the relationship between greater equality and economic growth. One of the most important obstacles to reducing income inequalities, and indeed one of the reasons why recent governments allowed them to grow, was the belief that inequality was a stimulus to effort and economic growth. For many years the conventional wisdom among economists was that we had to choose between equity and growth. Students in economics and the social sciences were taught that there was a trade-off between the two. Now, however, most of that has been swept away. There are at least four studies using independent data which suggest that more egalitarian societies have faster growth rates.[10] Indeed, the signs are of a new economic orthodoxy which says that equity is good for growth.[11] The shift in opinion has even started to percolate into the World Bank. Explanations of the association between equity and faster growth range from issues to do with the expense and wastage of 'human resources' caused by relative poverty and the failure to invest in people, to the ways in which trust and better social cohesion lubricate the workings of society so reducing firms' 'external costs'. Evidence for the view that inequality was good for growth was never strong, and the idea that a society can work efficiently while wasting the potential contribution of as much as a quarter or a third of its population is obviously absurd.

These changes in the empirical evidence and the new thinking are crucially important: they tell us not only that we do not face a choice between going under in the face of international competition or accepting the social costs of greater inequality, but also that our economic position is likely to improve as a result of tackling the social divisions in our society. If inequality and the destructive effects of relative poverty lower society's productivity, then the need for economic efficiency becomes a socially progressive force. Economic efficiency means raising educational standards throughout the population; it means improving social cohesion and ensuring that people are able to develop their productive potential.

What is true at the societal level may also be true in terms of the social organisation of work. Rather than reducing efficiency, a more cohesive and egalitarian ethos which improved working relationships seems likely to improve productivity. Consider the implications of a situation (shown in the Whitehall Studies) in which death rates are three times as high among the most junior as among the most senior office staff. What does it mean if sickness absence - whether for short spells or for longer medically certified spells - are six times as high among the most junior staff?[12] The problem for employers is twofold. It is not simply that poor health is expensive - though that should not be forgotten.

---

10. A. Glyn, D. Miliband (eds), *Paying for inequality: the economic cost of social injustice*, Rivers Oram Press, London 1994.
11. L. Osberg, 'The equity/efficiency trade-off in retrospect', *Canadian Business Economics*, Spring 1995.
12. F. North, S.L. Syme, A. Feeney *et al*, 'Explaining socioeconomic differences in sickness absence: the Whitehall II study', *British Medical Journal*, 1993.

It is also that the factors which provide the most powerful explanations of health differences at work are things like the amount of control people have over their work, their security, the social support they get from colleagues, their self-esteem, anger and depression. These are all quite closely related to morale, and it is likely that people are less productive where morale is low. For years it seemed that health inequalities research in the workplace was fundamentally inimical to business interests, but the truth is surely that they cannot afford to ignore it. Institutions need to recognise that employees will have better morale, will be healthier and will make a bigger contribution to the organisation's efficiency if they feel valued instead of used, and are able to combine a sense of purpose in their work with greater control over it.

Eventually this must go further than differences in management style. Although firms already try to foster a sense of commitment and loyalty in their staff, a structure of exploitative employer/employee relationships is surely ultimately incompatible with having a sense of purpose about one's work and feeling a valued member of a team. Is it too much of a flight of fantasy to imagine that finding a resolution to these issues will tend to favour firms which move closer to some form of industrial democracy? Is it an act of faith to believe that emancipated and purposeful human beings function better and that the institutional arrangements which foster their emancipation will have a competitive advantage?

It is important that the need to work largely within the market for the foreseeable future does not blind us to the social gains which may be possible within that framework. The astonishing flexibility of capitalism and the market means that they need not be incompatible with economic democracy (a term which can cover a wide range of institutional forms including the election of directors and chief executives by employees - essentially making bosses accountable to employees - to more cumbersome arrangements for involving employees more directly in decision making). Even within the market we are not necessarily stuck forever with private capital exercising exclusive control over the productive system. Already a great deal of capital is - like the pension funds - owned by institutions, and there are already examples of pension funds controlled by the members whose pension they manage. Nor is there any insurmountable obstacle to uncoupling sources of capital investment from ownership and control. Firms controlled democratically by employees would be perfectly capable of raising capital by paying agreed interest rates without having to give control to the providers of loans; and investors - whether institutions or private individuals - would be able to make their assessments of risk and act accordingly. One of the mysterious features of the 'debate' on the Labour Party's Clause IV is how it failed to turn into a debate about forms of democratic employee control - rather than control by either government or capital.

Despite the anti-social core of the market, there are numerous opportunities for social progress to which the market mechanism itself may not be an obstacle. It is important to distinguish between obstacles arising from the institutional power of the privileged and the effects of the market mechanism itself. Indeed the vested interests of the privileged often act as a brake on the more democratic tendencies in the market. It was this democratic aspect of the market which made Tom Paine see free trade as a counter to the institutionalised power of the aristocracy; and it perhaps explains why the rapid economic growth among the so-called Asian 'tiger' economies started only after the combined effects of the second world war and the struggle with communism had weakened or removed the previous ruling elites and ushered in a number of social reforms - including greater equality.

In the absence of an alternative to the market, the social fabric depends on the extent to which the market can be socialised. Few of the progressive features of market societies have come about directly as a result of the unfettered working of the market. Most have involved political organisation, trade unions, energetic campaigns and the use of legislative power. Objectives for the future, such as the democratisation of economic life, the development of humanistic and egalitarian working relationships, and more cohesive societies, are not only winnable within the prevailing system, but are made all the more urgent by the demands of economic efficiency. Without social reform, the market, guided only by the institutionalised power of the rich, would jeopardise not only the real quality of life but also the social and economic progress of our society.

In material practice we become ever more interdependent as we produce goods and services for the use of others and rely for the satisfaction of almost all our needs on what others - all over the world - produce. This social activity will need to be co-ordinated by the market until our sociality is sufficiently developed for us to be able to act directly in relation to the social purposes inherent in it. But it is surely imaginable that, as we grow to experience ourselves as gaining a sense of purpose from working on equal terms with others in a cohesive society we will also start being able to reduce reliance on the market in other areas. If so, the humanisation of society will depend more on pushing back the boundaries of the market, and on gradual increases in the range of our activities which are not mediated by the overtly self-interested and exploitative rationale of the cash nexus. By expanding the sphere of interactions which we experience as social, egalitarian and humanistic - rather than as anti-social market transactions - we will increase our social capacities, so paving the way for further advances and a fuller realisation of our human sociality.

There is now strong evidence from evolutionary psychology that we have genetically enshrined capacities for living co-operatively, based on relations of 'reciprocal altruism': a tendency to feel indebted, to reciprocate gifts, and to be intolerant of freeloaders.[13] The dominance of gift exchange and food sharing among hunter-gatherers depended on the power of the gift to create a sense of indebtedness and the need to make a return gift. These patterns of meaning are human characteristics found in all societies. But they extend more widely and more deeply than the aspects of reciprocity most directly involved in reciprocal gift exchange. Contributing to the welfare of others - whether within the family, among work colleagues, or in society more generally - brings with it a sense of having a role and a function in relation to others. It is an essential source of a sense of self-worth, of self-realisation in relation to others. Contributing voluntarily to the welfare of others is self-validating and provides a sense of meaning in a way which activity motivated by the self-interested rationale of the market often cannot. By turning an activity into a self-interested activity, payment tends to separate the actor from the inherent social purpose of the activity.

It is the unmediated and inherently social links which are most fundamentally inconsistent with the market. Our capacity for reciprocal altruism is the basis of social relations, and was once the basis of social organisation. Membership of the sharing group was also the nearest thing to a guarantee of security: it meant that you were not on your own, that others

---

13. M. Ridley, *The origins of virtue*, Viking 1996.

would come to your support when you faced difficulties - just as you were obligated to support them. It seems increasingly likely that the social environment most conducive to good health will turn out to be one in which people are bound together by relations of practical reciprocity, and daily life is organised in a way which makes more of that reciprocity apparent. The deep social needs illustrated by the health patterns with which this article started probably depend for their satisfaction on experiencing ourselves as part of a web of human relations providing mutual support through reciprocal altruism.

At the moment the main boundary between the areas of market exchange and sharing coincides with the boundary of the family or domestic household. We also have varying opportunities for reciprocity with friends and with colleagues at work. But always the form of exchange marks out the degree to which relationships are social. The sense of discord when what seem inherently social activities are commercialised shows the importance of the social meaning of different exchange systems.

Titmuss's work on blood donors indicates the potential for reciprocal altruism to find wider expression. An essential part of the socialisation of life involves expanding the areas of working life, and life on the streets, which are egalitarian and socially mediated. This includes not only areas like health services which are free to users, but also a huge range of voluntary work. It is not simply a matter of an intimate cocoon of social relationships for each of us; it is also a matter of social inroads into the public life of society, of finding ways of making the public space more of a social space. Perhaps provisions such as free urban public transport would serve to increase the sense of common citizenship.

The project of making modern societies more user-friendly is then partly a project of exploiting the unrealised social potential of the market, and of expanding the area of life which is not mediated by the market. The determinants of health contain a message about our social needs and our potential for social motivation, to which the institutions of our society must adapt.

The quality of the social environment is clearly the next big project facing developed societies. The increasing interest in ideas like stakeholding societies, communitarianism and social cohesion show how it is moving up the political agenda. There is now ample evidence that the real human benefits of continued economic growth are subject to sharply diminishing returns in the developed world. As well as posing environmental problems, further increases in absolute material standards are now less important to our subjective welfare than psychosocial factors influenced by income inequalities and the quality of social relations. As Robert Frank has shown, the individual desire for increased income is better understood as a desire to improve one's relative position in society than as a desire for economic growth with no change in relative position.[14] From this perspective, inequality remains a stimulus to economic growth even though growth itself can never satisfy the desires which lie behind it, to improve one's relative position. Even the discomfort of economic recessions is not really evidence of the importance of growth itself. We value booms not so much for the growth they bring, but because a by-product of that is a temporary decline in unemployment, in business bankruptcies and an increase in profits. To be permanently hooked on economic growth because it happens to provide a partial solution to problems of unemployment smacks of the junkie - there must be other solutions.

To say that we do not need economic growth as much as we did, or as poorer countries still do, does not mean an end to technical change. Instead it means thinking about qualitative rather than quantitative change. We need continued innovation partly to save resources and decrease the impact of economic activity on the environment. We also need innovation and qualitative improvements to deal with the incoherent material infrastructure of our society. But that need not involve quantitative growth. And, because it is a choice between sinking and swimming, we need to maintain international competitiveness. But let us at least feel fortified by the knowledge that that is consistent with the central project of improving the psychosocial quality of life throughout society.

14. R.H. Frank, *Choosing the right pond: human behavior and the quest for status*, Oxford University Press, Oxford 1996.

Soundings

Soundings is a journal of politics and culture. It is a forum for ideas which aims to explore the problems of the present and the possibilities for a future politics and society. Its intent is to encourage innovation and dialogue in progressive thought. Half of each issue is devoted to debating a particular theme: topics in the pipeline include: Active Welfare in Britain, America, and The European Left.

This book is a *Soundings* post-election special supplement FREE to subscribers, £4.99 in bookshops

Why not subscribe?
Make sure of your copy

Subscription rates, 1997 (3 issues)

INDIVIDUAL SUBSCRIPTIONS: UK - £35.00   *Rest of the World - £45.0*
INSTITUTIONAL SUBSCRIPTIONS UK - £70.00   *Rest of the World - £80.00*

Please send me one year's subscription starting with Issue Number _____

I enclose payment of £ _____

I wish to become a supporting subscriber and enclose a donation of £ _____

I enclose total payment of £ _____

Name _____

Address _____

_____

_____ Postcode _____

Please return this form with cheque or money order payable to Soundings and send to:

Soundings, c/o Lawrence & Wishart, 99A Wallis Road, London E9 5LN